The Bombay Brasserie
Cookbook

The Bombay Brasserie Cookbook

by Udit Sarkhel

Over 100 recipes with the
authentic flavours of the Raj

PAVILION

DEDICATED TO MR A. B. KERKAR, CHAIRMAN AND MANAGING
DIRECTOR, TAJ GROUP OF HOTELS

First published in Great Britain in 1996 by
PAVILION BOOKS LIMITED
26 Upper Ground, London SE1 9PD

Introduction © Ismail Merchant
General introduction © Pavilion Books Ltd
Recipes © Taj International Hotels (HK) Limited
Food photographs copyright © Vernon Morgan 1996
Drawings on page 9 reproduced by kind permission of Madame Holubowicz

Designed by David Fordham

A CIP catalogue record for this book is available from the British Library.

ISBN (hbk) 1 85793 886 0
ISBN (pbk) 1 85793 988 3

Typeset in Cochin by Servis Filmsetting Ltd, Manchester
Printed and bound in Spain by Bookprint

2 4 6 8 10 9 7 5 3 1

This book may be ordered by post direct from the publisher.
Please contact the Marketing Department. But try your bookshop first.

The Bombay Brasserie is part of Taj International Hotels (HK) Limited

CONTENTS

Introduction by Ismail Merchant

WHEN THE BOMBAY BRASSERIE opened in 1982 I was out of the country and therefore unable to accept the invitation to its inauguration: by the time I returned it seemed that everyone in London was talking about it. As a native of Bombay and a passionate cook I was curious to know what all the fuss was about, went there with some friends, and was immediately impressed by its cool, colonial style, by the efficiency and professionalism of the staff and, above all, by the food.

The Bombay Brasserie had suddenly rendered the ersatz plush-palace interiors and the generic 'curry' of conventional Indian restaurants in the West an anachronism. Here, at last, was a serious attempt to introduce occidental palates to the infinite variety and the complex tastes of Indian regional cuisine. Parsi, Goan, Bengali, Gujerati, North and South Indian, as well as Portuguese and Raj influences, were all represented in a menu which, in turn, represented the cultural diversity of Bombay itself.

That was quite an achievement, but in 1988 the Brasserie went even further by importing master chef Udit Sarkhel from the Taj Hotel in Bombay and the food at the Brasserie reached a level of refinement and creativity that would be hard to match anywhere. Like most gifted chefs Udit creates original dishes based on traditional principles, but he can also take a familiar recipe and by some alchemy make it entirely his own. In addition, he has introduced elements from his native Bihar which further extends the scope of his cooking. These

7

dishes, like everything Udit prepares, are based on domestic rather than commercial cookery, often using recipes that have been handed down from generation to generation.

The Bombay Brasserie has become a home away from home for me, and Adi Modi, the gracious General Manager who has been with the restaurant since it opened, will always somehow manage to find a table for me even if I have over-looked making a reservation and the place is packed to the roof. I bring all my friends here – Maggie Smith, Jeanne Moreau, Vanessa Redgrave, Anthony Hopkins, Simon Callow, Felicity Kendal, Tom Stoppard, Emma Thompson, Helena Bonham Carter, and of course my partners James Ivory and Ruth Prawer Jhabvala are among the many who have feasted on Udit's sensational deep-fried okra, his Goan fish curry, fish with green chutney in banana leaves, biryani, lamb chops baked in tandoori style – the list is endless.

On one occasion I even took over the whole restaurant for a party to celebrate the end of the shooting of our film *The Remains of the Day* and arranged for a belly dancer to come to entertain the guests. Hugh Grant, one of the stars of that film, was persuaded by the belly dancer to join her – he lost all his British inhibitions and made the evening even more memo-rable for everyone.

Since first coming to the Brasserie I have become more than a regular, and on each visit I am welcomed with the spirited enthusiasm of a cheer-leader by all the chefs working in the kitchen, by the waiters and wine waiters, and all the atten-dants – these, no less than Adi and Udit, have also contributed over the past fifteen years to make the Bombay Brasserie the place that it has become.

Ismail Merchant, 1996

The Bombay Brasserie

Adi Modi, General Manager of the Bombay Brasserie,
and Udit Sarkhel, Executive Chef

IN A ROOM DEEP IN THE TAJ HOTEL in downtown Bombay, Mr Sohoni, an astrologer of some reputation, pored over his charts. His task that day was not, for once, to cast the most auspicious date for the wedding of a daughter or of a first-born son. He had been instructed instead to provide the best possible dates for a birth, a birth that was to occur more than 4000 miles away, in London, England, at 51' 32' North, 0' 05' West, to be precise – and Mr Sohoni always was precise in these matters. Mr Sohoni analysed the position of the stars and the planets. Finally he prepared a list of dates that augured well. So it was that on the tenth of December 1982, with Sagittarius in the ascendant at dawn and Gemini at dusk, the Bombay Brasserie was born, in accordance with Mr Sohoni's instructions, just in time for the evening sitting.

If the succeeding years are anything to go by, restaurateurs might be well advised to consult Mr Sohoni before finalizing any births of their own. Feted by the critics and favoured by the guides, from its earliest days the Bombay Brasserie has been patronized by the great and the good, by the stars and the celebrities, and by those who come simply because they believe that the food it serves is the best of its kind in the world. The Brasserie has prospered through recession and survived the vicissitudes of fashion to become a London institution. It has led a charmed life.

All this for a restaurant that's as likely to serve you a dish based on a snack sold from a Bombay vendor's hand cart as one drawn from the sumptuous table of a Moghul emperor, a restaurant that introduced a menu quite untried in Britain, as rich, varied and cosmopolitan as the city after which the Brasserie is named. When you experience the cuisine of the Bombay Brasserie through the recipes in this cookbook, you are experiencing a taste of Bombay itself, savouring its history and its culture. So let us return to the place where it all started.

'THY TOWERS, THEY SAY, GLEAM FAIR,
BOMBAY, ACROSS THE BRIGHT BLUE SEA.'

BOMBAY TODAY is a vast and thriving metropolis of over nine million people, the commercial powerhouse of modern India. Delhi may be India's capital and administrative centre, Bangalore its new silicon valley, but it's in Bombay that the deals are still done. The city is, in fact, an island, on the western coast of the sub-continent, linked to the mainland by bridges – or rather, it's a series of seven islands, joined together over the last two centuries by landfills and drainage to create a peninsula 12 miles long by three miles broad at its widest point. Its shape curiously resembles Manhattan – although with four times the density of population. These days the real estate values in Bombay actually exceed Manhattan and are among the highest in the world.

Unlike Delhi, Bombay is not an ancient city. Until the sixteenth century, these islands were the palm-fringed outposts of the local Koli fishing people. Samphire grew across empty

saltwater marshes and small huts clustered on the shore. The mountains of the Western Ghats rose as a backdrop on the mainland. It was a beautiful, if, as the early European visitors were to discover to their cost, somewhat malarial spot. The Portuguese took possession of the islands as a small trading post in the sixteenth century. For many years it was believed that the name Bombay came from the Portuguese *buan bahia*, or 'good harbour'; now it is widely accepted that the name refers to Mumba Devi, the mouthless Hindu goddess whose idol was worshipped in the first temple on the islands.

The British, lured by the spice trade, arrived in the early 1600s in the ships of the East India Company. It was at Surat, to the north, where they set up their first 'factory', in fact a simple trading settlement. Bombay came into British possession in 1662, as part of the dowry of Catherine of Braganza to Charles II. It was promptly leased from the Crown by the East India Company for £10 in gold per annum. Easier to defend than Surat and blessed with a fine

10

natural harbour, the infant Bombay had its staunch supporters. Gerald Aungier, governor there from 1672–7, had great plans for a fine colonial city and actively encouraged all nationalities and religions to settle in the islands – a tradition that stood Bombay in good stead through the next three centuries. In those expansionist days, however, many British considered the town to be little more than a backwater: Samuel Pepys called it 'that poor little island'. The momentous events of the next century and a half in India all but passed it by. The Moghul dynasty rose and fell to the north. Colonial power was contested in the east, first around Madras where the East India Company fought the French for control of the region, then around Calcutta where Robert Clive – Clive of India – laid the foundations of the British Raj. All this was heard as distant thunder across the Ghats in Bombay. The people here were far too concerned with the much more serious business of making money.

Bombay was, from the first, a trader's town. The real activity was always in the godowns and warehouses, the counting houses, wharves and shipyards. The ships that Bombay built to carry its wares were among the finest in the world – the British Admiralty certainly thought so: it commissioned its first ever foreign-built vessels from Bombay, frigates that saw battle at Trafalgar. As the town grew it became the administrative centre of the Bombay Presidency, ultimately controlling Gujerat and Sind to the north, the Deccan to the east and Goa to the south. After the Indian Mutiny of 1857 the British Government did away with the last vestiges of the East India Company and declared direct sovereign rule from Britain. Queen Victoria became Empress of India, and the first Viceroy of the British Raj took up residence in Calcutta. Calcutta was the heart of British India – but Bombay was, increasingly, the pulse.

'OF NO MEAN CITY AM I!'

THE MID-NINETEENTH CENTURY thrust Bombay into the spotlight. The city was ready. The so-called 'overland route'

from England, via Egypt by steamer down the Nile, had cut the time and cost of travel between Bombay and Europe. By 1840, a passage to Bombay from Britain which had once cost £1000 could be had for as little as £100. Roads through the Presidency had been improved. The first railhead opened in the 1850s. Restrictive trading monopolies were swept away. Then, in 1861, the American War of Independence broke out, holding up the supply of raw cotton from the American south to the British mills. The price of Indian cotton in Bombay duly soared, and in the 'cotton mania' of 1862–5 fortunes were made and lost.

By the time the dust had settled, Bombay was acquiring all the trappings of a grand city in the Victorian mould. It was hailed in Britain as the Manchester and Liverpool of the East. Great public buildings were erected, in a style that came to be known as Indian Gothic, a rich amalgam of towers and cupolas. Many of them, like Sir Gilbert Scott's University and F. W. Stevens's magnificent Victoria Terminus, still stand, making Bombay, in the words of architectural writer Gavin Stamp, 'the finest Gothic city in the world'. Rudyard Kipling, born in Bombay in 1865 to a sculptor father who encouraged native workmen to embellish these very buildings, was to write with pride years later: 'Surely in toil or fray/Under an alien sky/Comfort it is to say/Of no mean city am I!'

Imperial Bombay was a melting pot fired by the interests of commerce. In its streets and markets were furniture makers from Sindh, cobblers from China, peddlers from Gujerat, merchants from Persia, Arab horse dealers, Armenians, Jesuits, Brahmins, Jains, Fakirs, Europeans, Baghdad Jews, each with their distinctive dress and customs. Even the ruling British society in Bombay was a little less starched and a little more tolerant than in Calcutta. As one native Bombayite on a lecture tour of England in the 1860s told his rapt audience: 'Passing through the streets of Bombay presents a magnificent, varied, curious, animated, original and unparalleled moving panorama of manners, costumes and races not presentable in any other quarter of the globe.' The British might have declared themselves the sovereign government of India, but in Bombay other imperatives held sway. A new native aristocracy arose, one not based on the blood lines of lords or maharajahs, but on empires of cotton, iron and steel, shipping and trade. They built magnificent Gothic mansions along Bombay's newly reclaimed seafronts and on the exclusive heights of Malabar Hill. They were the princes of the city.

THE RISE OF THE PARSIS

PRE-EMINENT AMONG THE NEW ARISTOCRACY were the Parsis, who came originally from Persia. Followers of the prophet Zoroaster, their religion was founded on the seeking of knowledge through the worship of fire and sun. In the ancient world they were seen as a wise race, a race apart – the Magi, the Three Wise Men of the Christian nativity legend, were Parsis. Around 650AD, the Parsis left Persia to escape religious persecution. Their epic wanderings ended in 745AD when they landed at Sanjan in Gujarat, on the north-west coast of India. Here they remained, assimilating the language of Gujerat but retaining their own religion and customs.

When the British came to India, a special relationship grew swiftly between them and the Parsis, first in Surat and later in Bombay, where the Parsis settled in increasing numbers, building their Fire Temples and swiftly mastering the English tongue. Parsis developed a formidable reputation in business and became the pillars of Bombay's trading, shipbuilding and banking industries. By 1850, Parsis owned half of Bombay island. Many wealthy Parsis increasingly modelled themselves on the British, dressing in Western clothes, playing golf and cricket, and sending their children to Oxford and Cambridge. The first ice creams in Bombay would have been consumed at a Parsi dinner party. The first private motor cars would have had a Parsi behind the wheel. Jamshetji Jeejeebhoy was the first Indian to be made a baronet. His family, along with families like the Wadias, the

Camas, and in particular the Tatas, were instrumental in creating modern Bombay.

THE TATAS AND THE TAJ

JAMSHETJI NUSSERWANJI TATA (1839–1904) first made his money in the cotton trade. He survived the cotton mania to build an empire of mills, steel works, iron ore mines, shipping and real estate. He died while on a tour of Europe, and is buried at Brookwood in Surrey. The Tata dynasty continued to flourish, moving into tea, trucks and scientific research. The Tatas are the only private individuals in the world to have owned their own nuclear reactor. Air India started life as a Tata company. There is even an entire Tata-run city. The tradition of philanthropy which had always characterized the Parsis in Bombay continues, with the Tata Group donating one-third of its profits to charity.

For any visitor to Bombay, however, the most conspicuous jewel of the Tata empire is the Taj Mahal Hotel, which stands facing the sea opposite the Gate of India, the triumphal arch originally built to welcome King George V on his visit to India in 1911. The Taj is a huge and imposing building of cupolas, arches and gables. The story goes that J. N. Tata had once arranged to meet a business colleague at Watson's Hotel on the Esplanade, then the most up-market place in Bombay. On his arrival, he was refused entry because he was a native. He swore that he would build his own hotel and put them to shame.

The Taj was completed in 1903. Watson's days as a hotel ceased long ago. There is a colourful tale about the Taj's design, too: it's said that the architect, an Englishman named Chambers, had planned for the gardens to be at the front of the hotel, but that the builders had put the thing together back to front. When he first saw the completed building, the architect is said to have rushed to the fifth floor and flung himself off in despair. There's no truth to it – in fact, having the gardens behind the hotel simply follows the Indian model. There was one dramatic exit that the Taj did witness,

however. Had you been staying in one of the favoured waterfront rooms in the Taj on 15th August 1947, you would have had a grandstand view of the last British troops parading through the arch to their ships. Having seen the beginnings of British power in India, Bombay also saw the very end of it, as the sun finally set on the Raj, leaving India to its hard won Independence.

THE NEW GLEAMING TOWERS

TODAY, launches no longer tie up at the pier opposite the Taj to disgorge their expectant travellers into the heat of the Bombay sun. The visitor is more likely to take the long and sometimes frustrating 34km drive in from the airport. The twentieth century has altered the face of Bombay, and vast suburbs now sprawl on the mainland north of the peninsula. But the personality of the place remains the same. Now capital of the state of Maharashtra, it is still India's most cosmopolitan city, attracting people from every part of the

sub-continent and beyond. Goans, Gujeratis, Bengalis, South Indians from Tamil Nadu and Kerala, Maharashtrans from the small towns and villages inland all come, seeking their fortune (or at least a living), and each contributing a little of their own culture as part of their bargain with the city.

Even the counting houses are still there – it's just that today they are the steel and glass skyscrapers of Dalal Street, the modern business district. The city is home to the very poor, as well as the very rich in their mansions up on Malabar Hill. These days, though, the wealthy elite are as likely to be film producers or movie stars from Bollywood, the huge movie industry based in Bombay that turns out the all singing, all dancing Hindi spectaculars so beloved in India.

The 600-room Taj Hotel, still owned by the Tatas, remains the finest hotel in the city. Today it is the flagship of the Taj Group, which now owns luxury hotels across the world. In 1981, the Group's ever-extending feelers reached a rather run-down hotel in London called Bailey's, close to

Gloucester Road underground station. As it stood, the hotel urgently needed extensive renovation. But it was blessed with a large, airy breakfast room of particularly pleasing proportions. At this point, the Taj group had an idea that brings us right back to Mr Sohoni's augury. Why not open a restaurant in London which served the cuisine of Bombay? This was the brainchild of Camellia Panjabi, then Executive Director of the Group. But it begged a very big question. What exactly was Bombay cuisine?

DHANSAKS AND DABBAWALLAHS

EACH COMMUNITY THAT CAME TO BOMBAY brought its cooking with it. Even the British, who in the early years of the East India Company would happily eat the delicious *biryanis* and *pillaos* of the local Indian cooks, increasingly turned to their own cuisine, often poorly cooked with incorrect ingredients in an unsuitable climate. Writers of manners often disparaged the Anglo-Indian table, groaning as it did with boiled and roasted meats – 'hecatombs of slaughtered animals', as one put it. Of course, Anglo-Indian food during the Raj included some famous signature dishes that became part of the British culinary heritage – dishes like mulligatawny soup, kedgeree, the chicken dish Country Captain and the common-or-garden curry. But after the Indian Mutiny, 'native' food went right out of vogue. More often than not, the sahib and memsahib in their Raj villa would be tucking into a Sunday tiffin of clear soup, fried fish, roast beef and Yorkshire pudding, perhaps garnished with a bottled sauce bought from one of the provisions stores. Meanwhile, out in the streets, in the bazaars, at weddings, at feasts, in mansions, in temples and in tens of thousands of ordinary households a veritable cornucopia of Indian cuisine was being lovingly prepared and eaten.

The range of food available today in Bombay is, if anything, greater than ever. It is woven into the fabric of society far more than in the West. There are religious imperatives, of course. For Hindus the cow is sacred. Many Hindus are vegetarians, either completely, or on certain days of the month. The Jains will eat nothing that grows beneath the earth – including onions, ginger and garlic. Some communities have periods of fasting. The holy book of the Parsis – the *Vendidad* – advises their community against fasting.

At bustling Crawford Market in the heart of town Bombayites of every persuasion come to buy their fresh meat, fish and vegetables. The cool stone halls, built in 1861, are decorated with reliefs by Lockwood Kipling, Rudyard's father. The market is packed with produce from the four corners of India.

Housewives or husbands on their way home from work pick their way through the heaving stalls and the scurrying chickens and goats – a Goan selecting a cut of pork for a *vindaloo* and seeking out the potent Goan chilli to spice it; a Parsi buying eggs for the delicate sauce of the fish dish *Saas Ni Macchi*, a Gujerati selecting the plumpest *brinjal* (aubergine), to be sliced and pan-fried in a hot and sweet paste to make *Brinjal Kalwa*.

Each lunchtime, a phenomenon occurs that brings together two of Bombay's favourite occupations – eating and entrepreneurialism. This is the Bombay *dabbawallah* system. An office worker has a job in downtown Bombay. In their block of flats in the sprawling suburbs on the mainland, his wife – the majority of women still stay at home while their husbands go out to work – will pack his lunch into a stainless steel container called a *dabba*. The first *dabbawallah* picks it up from their door mid-morning and takes it, along with a hundred others all carefully numbered and coded, teetering on a pushcart to the local railway station. There it joins many hundreds more in a compartment until it reaches Churchgate or Victoria Terminus in central Bombay. Yet another *dabbawallah* reads the code number or name and takes it on a trolley to its destination. And there, at twelve o'clock, tiffin arrives. The reverse process takes the empty box all the way back. In this way, literally tens of thousands of workers get their home-cooked food fresh every lunchtime.

Then there are the restaurants. Even the snootiest inhabitant of Delhi envies Bombay its restaurants. Here a crowded South Indian emporium preparing *dosas*, rice pancakes stuffed with a potato mixture and served with coconut chutney. There an air conditioned place with darkened windows where businessmen tuck into a rich, red, North Indian *Rogan Josh*. In a Muslim part of town, stalls in the evening cook kebabs on the street and dish them out in a roll of bread. A Bengali sweetmeat shop in Kemp's Corner does a roaring trade. In a dark Irani cafe they are serving the Parsi *dhansak*, chicken or lamb cooked with lentils and vegetables and spiced sweet and sour. Down at Chowpatty, by the ocean, snack vendors at their carts serve up *sev puris* and *gol gappas*, vegetarian snacks smothered in spicy and sweet sauces.

THE BRASSERIE AND THE GREAT BRITISH CURRY

THE TAJ GROUP'S IDEA was to present London with the authentic food of Bombay in all its ethnic variety. The cooking would be of the finest quality, prepared with the freshest ingredients, and priced accordingly. The chefs would be from the kitchen of the Bombay Taj, which boasted perhaps the best restaurant in Bombay, the Tanjore. It would be served plated – that is, diners would not be sharing main dishes as was the curry-house tradition in Britain. Each main dish would come, as it might in a Bombay home, with a side dish of *dal* (lentils) and *subzi* (vegetables).

All this was revolutionary to the British curry-eater, who was more than a little set in his ways. In his excellent book, *The Raj At Table* , David Burton points out that in general the cultural traffic between Britain and India has been very much one way, leaving the sub-continent with, among other things, a love of forms completed in triplicate, a lot of British architecture and a passion for cricket. The exception has been food. The British made almost no impact on Indian eating habits; Indians have made a huge impact on the

British, almost all of it felt in the last 50 years. The first Indian restaurant opened in London in 1926. Two more had opened by the end of the War. By 1960 there were around 300.

The earlier restaurants were run by Punjabis and served north Indian fare, with the rich *kormas* and *biryanis* of Moghul cookery to the fore. This became the standard curry house menu, and it caught on. After a long period of post-war austerity, Britons liked the new Indian restaurants, with their extravagant decor, attentive service and low prices. By the end of the 1960s there were 1200 curry houses. The running of the burgeoning Indian restaurant business had by now been taken over by a people from a part of the sub-continent that was once East Bengal, became East Pakistan and finally achieved independence as Bangladesh. Strictly speaking, they were not Indians at all. Neverthless, these Bangladeshi proprietors continued to cook the established menu, an approximation of North Indian food which had developed a life of its own. Many dishes were prepared by adding the principal ingredients to a standard curry sauce, varied for chilli hotness. *Korma* meant mild, *madras* hotter and *vindaloo* extra fiery. In no way was it authentic: in India, a *korma* can be mild or spicy, a *vindaloo* is a Goan pork dish and a *madras* simply doesn't exist (except as Madras curry powder).

The high street curry house might be a lore unto itself but the British have taken it to their hearts. By 1980, there were over 3000. Today, according to figures from the British Curry Club, there are about 8000, most of them Bangladeshi-run. Over 2.5 million British diners a week eat out at Indian restaurants, spending up to £2 billion a year. Fads and fashions have periodically spiced up the business. Tandoor cooking swept the nation when it arrived in the UK. In the 1990s, *baltis*, prepared in a wok-like dish resembling a *karai*, took off. The consumption of a *vindaloo* or an even more chilli-hot *phal*, usually after consuming several pints of lager, was part of the initiation to manhood of every self- respecting British male.

In this market, the Taj Group's plans for the Bombay Brasserie demanded pause for thought. Would the British go for the authentic cuisine of Bombay? Who had heard of Parsi cooking, for example? Would they pay the prices? The menu was not the only revolutionary thing, either; there was *that name*. Bombay, yes. But Brasserie? Indian restaurants in 1982 were called things like Koh-I-Nor, Star of India or Tandoori Nights. They were not called Brasseries, replete as the word is with Gallic images of bustling *sommeliers* and clinking wine glasses. Adi Modi, who was summoned literally from his bed in the Taj Group's Sheba Hotel in the Yemen to oversee the opening of the restaurant as General Manager and who still wields control today, says: 'The name caused some controversy in the House of Tatas. The late J. R. D. Tata, our chairman, felt that the word was entirely inappropriate for a top-class Indian restaurant. But Camellia Panjabi, whose brainchild the whole thing was, insisted. After all, it was to be a Brasserie in every sense – the space, the ambience, the menus, the separate wine and cocktail list.'

Indian food, Brasserie-style – in a neo-colonial ambience. The lofty space of the Bailey's Hotel breakfast room was transformed into a Raj-style Gymkhana. The word means, literally, 'ball-house'. At the height of the Raj, it signified a sports clubhouse, a place where the expatriate community gathered on verandas, listened to the whack of willow on leather and sipped their punch. The Bombay Gym, founded in 1875, still flourishes. To recreate the effect at the Bombay Brasserie, cane peacock chairs from Assam were brought in to furnish the cocktail bar. The original Victorian plaster-work ceiling was restored and touched up in pink, gold and eggshell blue. The walls were hung with paintings and prints of Parsi life in Bombay. Large, swishing ceiling fans were installed. The tables were laid with 98 elegant place settings. Plants, hanging and potted, palm and fern, were in profusion (the Brasserie today spends £10,000 a year caring for its greenery). A grand piano was moved in. The year after the opening a beautiful crescent-shaped conservatory was added, the most glamorous of settings in the evening.

THE BEST INDIAN RESTAURANT IN THE COUNTRY?

THE BOMBAY BRASSERIE opened without advertising and served 38 covers on its first evening. All the first day's takings were given to charity. The day after the first glowing review appeared four days later, the restaurant served 94 covers and, says Adi Modi, 'it hasn't looked back since'. Paul Levy of *The Observer* praised the authenticity of the food and hailed it as 'absolutely the best Indian restaurant in the country'. Fay Maschler in the *Evening Standard* wrote: 'The Bombay Brasserie brought with it a sweep of grandeur and an intelligible interpretation of the regionality of Indian cooking and at a stroke altered the preconceptions of a cuisine that had long been immured in yards of flock wall-paper and all-purpose sauces.'

That the launch coincided with a revival of interest in all things Raj was a fortuitous bonus. Films like *Jewel in the Crown*, *Heat and Dust* and *Gandhi* turned the spotlight on the days of Empire, and British India was suddenly fashionable. Before long, the Bombay Brasserie was being mentioned by the media in the same breath as some of London's chicest eateries – Langan's Brasserie, the Dorchester Grill, Harvey's. Its crescent-shaped conservatory was used for fashion shoots. Its buffet Sunday lunch swiftly established itself as an institution. It merited glowing reports in the food guides for its cooking and was also beginning to feature in the gossip pages as a favoured venue for writers, models, musicians, actors, businesspeople and politicians. On a busy evening the street outside was lined with Rolls Royces and Bentleys. Today, Adi Modi shakes his head with a smile. 'We were sure it would be a success, but we never expected it to be *such* a success.'

THE STARS COME OUT

STARGAZING has always been part of the Bombay Brasserie's appeal. On one night in 1988, gossip columnist Nigel Dempster reported spotting Bruce Springsteen, Charlton Heston, Telly Savalas, Ali MacGraw and Barbara Dickson all breaking *naan* here. Rock stars are well represented. Mick Jagger hired the conservatory for Jerry Hall's 35th birthday. David Bowie and Iman have done the same. Paul and Linda McCartney have been in and the Brasserie has catered for three parties at George Harrison's country estate. Terry Wogan, a long-term regular, once sent Stevie Wonder along after an interview. The singer took over the piano after dinner and treated his fellow guests to an hour-long impromptu concert.

Actors have always favoured the glamour of the Brasserie and its stock is high in Hollywood. All of the Godfathers – Pacino, De Niro and Brando – have forsaken pasta for a *pillao* here. Faye Dunaway, a regular, was once spotted passing a note of admiration across the restaurant to fellow diner Sir Lawrence Olivier. On the right evening, you might have taken your seat next to Kurt Russell and Goldie Hawn, Tom Hanks or Billy Crystal. Michael Caine, co-owner of Langan's in Piccadilly, once proclaimed that he liked to take lunch in his own Brasserie and dinner at the Bombay version. Sir Anthony Hopkins has been known, like many of the Brasserie's regulars, to treat the place more like a club, spending a couple of hours here with a newspaper at lunchtime then returning in the evening to discuss a project with a Hollywood executive. Whether the conversation over a tandoori mixed grill ever extended to the culinary preferences of Dr Hannibal Lecter, we just don't know. Ismail Merchant, the producer of the award-winning Merchant Ivory movie team and an acclaimed cookery author in his own right, is a close friend, frequently introducing his actors and actresses – Emma Thompson, Jeanne Moreau, Helena Bonham-Carter – to the Brasserie.

The sporting connections of the old Raj gymkhanas have been continued. From the world of cricket, Sir Gary Sobers, Ian Botham, Richie Benaud, Kapil Dev, Sunny Gavaskar, Imran Khan and the entire Australian squad (three times); from football, Terry Venables and Gary Lineker; during the

Wimbledon season, Connors, McEnroe and Navratilova. The restaurant has some powerful business allies, too: Sir Richard Greenbury, chairman of Marks and Spencer, eats here at least once a month, and both David Sainsbury and Richard Branson have been regulars. Royalty has been catered for; Prince and Princess Michael of Kent have eaten here, and the kitchens have cooked for the Prince of Wales, providing a vegetarian banquet for the Prince's Trust in 1992. There's no record of Prime Minister John Major coming here himself, despite his professed fondness for Indian food. But the John Major Lamb Curry Club, set up by a group of MPs after Major's trade visit to India in 1993, was launched at the Brasserie, which recreated for the occasion the *Dum Ka Kid Gosht* eaten with such relish by the PM at the Taj Bombay. Even fellow chefs have confessed that the Brasserie is a favourite place to come and eat when they doff their whites. Anton Mosimann is a long-term supporter and swaps menu tips with executive chef Udit Sarkhel.

Although the Bombay Brasserie is most decidedly not a take-away, even this service has been provided on occasions. Michael Barrymore orders them by phone to be sent to his house. The Sultana of Brunei has confessed to doing the same from the Dorchester. King of the take-away, however, is Hollywood star Tom Cruise. A regular at the Brasserie, along with his wife Nicole Kidman, when his shooting schedule on films like *Dracula* has brought him to London, Cruise would sometimes send a car to pick up a take-away for himself and the film crew out on location. On one occasion, Cruise placed a substantial order by phone. The food was prepared and put in a waiting car, which promptly drove to the airport. The food was loaded into a private jet which then flew to Italy. The location shoot was, it transpired, in Rome. Mr Modi still worries whether the rice was in top condition on arrival.

The Bombay Brasserie has been hugely influential. Today there is more interest in authentic Indian regional cooking than ever before. There is also a general acceptance that Indian food can, at its best, match any other cuisine in the world. As Loyd Grossman wrote in *The Sunday Times*: 'The rise of the flockless Indian restaurant must be one of the great socio-gastronomic tales of postwar Britain. But it was the opening of the Bombay Brasserie in 1982 which marked the apotheosis into *haute cuisine* of the London Indian restaurant.'

THE BOMBAY BRASSERIE KITCHEN

EXECUTIVE CHEF UDIT SARKHEL runs a team of seven chefs, all, like him, trained by the Taj Group in India. All the chefs in the kitchen are expert in their own fields. The Goan chef, a lady affectionately known as Auntie, has cooked this food all her life. There are tandoori, Parsi, north and south Indian specialists. One chef will always be doing vegetarian dishes in a completely separate kitchen – this is important for Indian religious reasons and the Brasserie likes to maintain that tradition.

There is some specialized equipment here. Most obvious are the large tandoor ovens that stand in the corner. Essentially, a tandoor is a huge round clay pot that tapers at the top to a neck and an opening. There is an opening near the base in which charcoal stands. Because the pot is fragile, it is usually protected by a brick or metal box (originally, it would be buried in the earth).

The hottest part of the tandoori is near the top, where the bread is usually cooked. In India, you'll find three sizes of tandoors: 15 breads, 22 or 25, the bread being a standard size. Temperatures are controlled by opening and closing the top or the bottom aperture – it's quite an art. The tandoor at the Brasserie never goes out – it is burning or smouldering 24 hours a day.

There is also a mammoth stone grinding machine. Using stone is traditional in the preparation of pastes and masalas and helps to keep the temperature of the grinding low – this is particularly important with coconut, which otherwise tends to separate. The machine is from Gajanan Grinders – the name relates to an elephant. Its big motor drives a

massive wheel weighing one ton. The granite stone that sits inside weighs another half a ton and has to be lifted for cleaning. It has a very slow grinding action, to produce a whole range of masalas, and even make lentil paste for *dosas* or *idlis*.

Over the years the availability of authentic Indian spices has improved enormously. Nevertheless, the Brasserie still imports Kashmiri and Goan chillis to ensure the correct colour and flavour of its dishes. These come in massive hessian sacks of 25 kilos each. Transport costs from India are twice the net cost of the chillis. Fortunately, other ingredients are generally available in the UK, but according to Chef Sarkhel, the water content of raw produce in the UK is greater than in India. 'Onions in India are quite dry and English onions were found to go rather soggy when browned. Now we use Spanish Improvers, which we hold here for four or five days to make them nice and crisp – the skin is crackly when you peel them. They compare very well with what we use in India.'

RECREATING THE BOMBAY BRASSERIE AT HOME

NONE OF THE INGREDIENTS for the recipes in this book should pose a problem to a domestic cook. Almost everything in the way of spices, pulses and rice should be available these days in good supermarkets. For that reason, we haven't included a detailed spice glossary. If there is anything slightly unusual in a recipe, it is mentioned in the text.

You can cook Indian food perfectly well without any specialized equipment. There are, however, one or two things that will make life a little easier for you. A *karahi* may be useful. This is a heavy-gauge two-handled Indian wok. The advantage of this is that, like a wok, you use far less oil. They are also quite convenient for deep frying. A *tawa* is a flat griddle used for cooking breads, and even shallow-frying fish or meat. It is again of a heavy gauge and retains heat without burning the food. You can always use a heavy omelette pan instead. You'll need a pastry board and rolling

pin for bread. An electric coffee mill and a blender will save you a lot of time grinding spices, but you might like to have a mortar and pestle as well. Try to get a small granite one rather than the ceramic version. Wooden ones are useless, except for show. For curries, get a deep saucepan with a heavy bottom made of stainless steel. It's essential that it is heavy bottomed or you will burn the curry. Even supermarkets now stock these. You also need one with a tight fitting lid that can go in the oven. Invest in a proper rice colander rather than use a sieve for draining rice. This will help you get the water out very quickly – if rice is in hot water for a minute too long it could be overcooked.

Build up a good selection of whole and ground spices (for advice on which ones see page 10) as well as your own spice mixtures. Udit Sarkhel has this tip: 'At home I don't use spice racks as I find they get oily and greasy. Instead I store my spice jars in a round biscuit tin and label them from the top. When I prepare Indian food, I always get out my chopping board and blender, cut the meats, chop the vegetables, and measure all my spices and ingredients out into glass bowls before I start. Only then I heat the oil and start cooking. It may take me ten minutes more, but it means I'm not in a mad rush and I don't burn anything.'

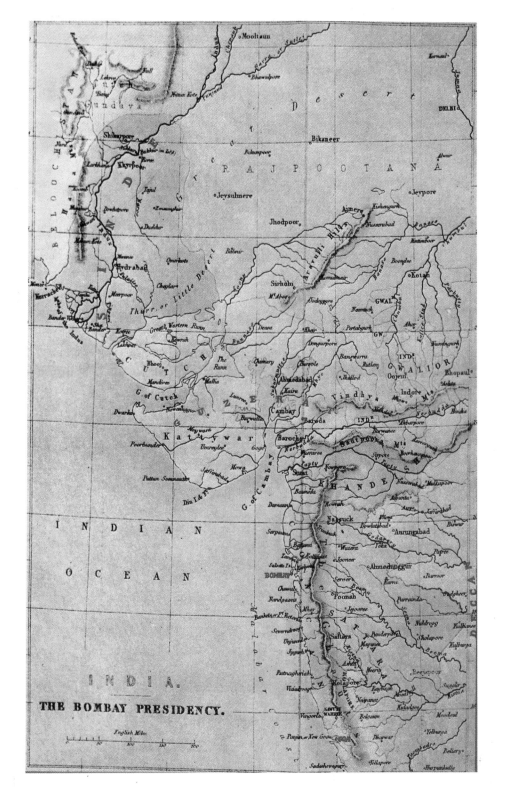

THE BOMBAY PRESIDENCY.

English Miles

Tindli,
Yellow Tomatoes
and Limes on Sea Salt

What you need for your Indian Kitchen

THIS CHAPTER IS ALL ABOUT *MIS-EN-PLACE*. Sound *mis-en-place* is the secret behind a cool-headed, smiling chef. *Mis-en-place* simply means pre-preparation and a practical plan of work. Indian cooking can be quite laborious and time-consuming if you have to grind all the required pastes and masalas before preparing a dish, so it is imperative that you keep the most commonly used pastes, combinations of spices and semi-processed ingredients ready at hand. If you don't cook Indian food very often, it may not be worth the trouble, but the optimistic view I take is that if you do have a back-up of pastes and masalas you certainly would be tempted to cook Indian more often. Maybe you could even do an Indian menu once a week.

Pre-preparation of ingredients is effective when they are stored in the correct way to give them maximum shelf-life in prime condition. You should also consider the important fact that spices and ingredients like onions and garlic are very strongly flavoured and aromatic. Airtight containers work both ways: the fresh aroma and texture of the paste is retained and at the same time other, more delicate foods such as milk or eggs do not become tainted. Old jam jars or similar containers work well, but you could buy a number of small identical jars to label and fill. They could then be arranged in round tins and stored in the spice cupboard or refrigerator.

In addition to the following recipes to follow for your *mis-en-place*, there are a lot of ready-prepared spice mixtures you can buy. The most commonly used off-the-rack mixtures include: *chaat masala, channa masala, sambar masala* and *dhansak masala*. These are available in Indian supermarkets and Thai and Chinese grocers, and it is much more convenient to buy them ready made than to grind and mix them yourself. In addition to these mixtures you should also keep spices ready in their natural, whole form, for example, cumin seeds, mustard seeds, coriander seeds, and in their ground form, such as ground turmeric, coriander, cumin and chilli powder – just to name a few. Buy them in small quantities to keep them fresh and replenish them often. With good *mis-en-place* I wish you happy cooking.

MASALAS

THESE GROUND SPICE COMBINATIONS are used for specific dishes, and each imparts its own unique flavour. Once it was very difficult to get these outside of India, and chefs would buy hordes of spices and painstakingly grind them by hand before setting off on any overseas travels. Today, however, it is possible to get all the major spices at Asian and Indian food shops. The most commonly used shop-bought spice mixtures include chaat masala, channa masala, sambar masala and dhansak masala.

GARAM MASALA ⓥ
Ground Whole Spice Mix

THE SECRET OF 'that special touch' in most Indian dishes is often the finely ground combination of spices called garam masala. Its balance of aroma, flavour and colour varies from chef to chef, and this is my favourite combination. We make this up in bulk at the Brasserie every three or four days. I assemble the spices and leave them on the side of the *tandoor* to dry, rather than dry-roasting them, as I suggest in this recipe for home cooks.

Unlike whole spices, which are usually fried in oil at the beginning of the cooking, this powder is almost always added just as a dish finishes cooking so the fresh aroma is preserved. In fact, this masala should always be used sparingly because it is so aromatic and it can easily over-power other flavours in the dish. It is important that the mixture just adds flavour and aroma but doesn't colour the gravy.

MAKES 12–15 TABLESPOONS
30 green cardamom pods
15 cloves
5 black cardamom pods
4 pieces of mace

four 2.5 cm/1 inch pieces of cinnamon sticks
5 tablespoons cumin seeds
2 tablespoons coriander seeds
1 tablespoon fennel seeds
1 teaspoon black peppercorns
½ teaspoon fenugreek seeds

PLACE ALL THE SPICES in a dry frying pan/skillet and heat over a very low heat, stirring constantly. As soon as the aroma from the spices begins wafting up, remove the pan from the heat. This step is to release the aromatic oils from the spice, not necessarily to add colour, although the seeds become browner.

Working with only a small quantity at a time, put the spices in an electric spice mill, blender or pestle and grind until a fine powder forms. Remove the cardamom pod skins. (If you've used a coffee grinder, instead of a grinder reserved just for spices, remember not to use it again for grinding coffee beans, or you will be serving masala coffee!) Allow to cool.

Store the garam masala in an air-tight container. As long as the container is tightly closed after each use, the masala should last for a long time.

JAVITRI, JAIPHAL AND ELAICHI MASALA Ⓥ
Mace, Nutmeg and Green Cardamom Powder

THE NAME OF THIS SPICE COMBINATION may sound long, but this is actually very simple to prepare. I use this mixture for more subtly and delicately flavoured kebabs and kormas. My experience of using this powder is that it has a tenderizing effect on meats, especially red meats. A recipe with just a touch of ginger, garlic and coarsely ground black peppercorns in it is perfectly complemented by this masala, which adds extra flavour.

Many cooks just blend the mace with the cardamom, but I prefer to add some nutmeg as well. Although mace and nutmeg are from the same family of spices, they have different qualities – mace has more aromatic oils, while the nutmeg gives the powder more body, as well as a sharp nutty flavour. If you are not familiar with mace, it is the lacy cocoon that covers the small, hard nutmeg. Both spices are usually sold separately.

MAKES ABOUT 225 G/8 OZ
100 g/4 oz mace
100 g/4 oz green cardamom pods
4 whole nutmegs

WARM THE SPICES under a preheated grill, without letting the colours change. Transfer to an electric spice mill, blender or pestle and blend until a fine powder forms. This powder tends to be a bit oily, but that is a sign of good-quality spices. Allow to cool.

Store the powder in an air-tight container.

PISA HUWA ADRAK AUR LASAN Ⓥ
Ginger and Garlic Paste
SEE PHOTOGRAPH ON PAGE 30

THIS FULL-FLAVOURED PASTE keeps very well in an air-tight jar in the refrigerator, so there really isn't any point in making it up in a smaller quantity. It is used in numerous recipes throughout this book, and it is also useful for basting a whole leg of lamb before roasting.

At The Bombay Brasserie we make this with equal quantities of ginger and garlic, but you can vary the proportion to suit your taste. The variations below of all-garlic and all-ginger pastes are also useful.

Freezing the paste in ice-cube trays, like ice cubes, is very useful. Once the cubes are solid, transfer them from the tray to a freezerproof bag. Whenever you want some paste, just remove a single cube. Be sure the bag is tightly sealed, however, or everything in the freezer will smell of ginger and garlic.

MAKES ABOUT 900 G/2 LB
450 g/1 lb fresh root ginger, peeled and chopped
450 g/1 lb garlic cloves, peeled

PLACE THE GINGER and garlic in a blender or food processor and process until a smooth paste forms, adding just enough water to help blend the ingredients, rather than dilute them. Store the paste in a jar with a tight-fitting lid in the refrigerator for up to 2 weeks, or freeze for up to 3 months.

VARIATIONS

GINGER PASTE Place 450 g/1 lb chopped peeled fresh root ginger in a blender or food processor and process until a smooth paste forms, adding just enough water to help blend the ginger, rather than dilute it.

GARLIC PASTE Place 450 g/1 lb peeled garlic cloves in blender or food processor and process until a smooth paste forms, adding just enough water to help blend the garlic, rather than dilute it.

TALA HUWA PYAZ ⓥ
Fried Brown Onions

SEE PHOTOGRAPH ON PAGE 31

THESE FRIED GOLDEN BROWN ONIONS add colour to gravies and are used to garnish many dishes. The important thing to remember is to remove the onions from the oil while they are very light golden brown. The fibres in them will continue 'cooking' as the onions cool and as this happens the slices will darken. The problem with many home-cooked biryanis is that they are garnished with dark brown onions because they were in the oil for too long.

MAKES ABOUT 450 G/1 LB/3 CUPS
450 g/1 lb/3 cups onions, thinly sliced
1 teaspoon salt
about 5 tablespoons vegetable oil

PLACE THE ONIONS in a bowl, sprinkle with the salt and leave for 3–4 minutes. Squeeze out the extra juice using the palm of your hand. This is an important step to extract the water in them. Heat the oil in a large frying pan/skillet until it is 180°C/350°F, or until a cube of bread browns in about 45 seconds. Add the onions and fry, stirring constantly, for 3½–4 minutes until they are light golden brown. Remove with a slotted spoon and leave to cool and darken on crumpled kitchen paper/paper towel. You can keep these in an airtight container for up to 10 days at room temperature.

PREVIOUS SPREAD, clockwise from bottom left (in bowls): chillies; raw coconut; grated coconut; Panch Phoran (*page 33*); Ginger and Garlic Paste (*page 29*); Fried Brown Onions (*page 32*); mace, nutmeg and cardamom powder; tamarind pulp (*page 33*).

TAZA NARIAL KA DOODH ⓥ
Coconut Milk

THIS IS A VERY USEFUL INGREDIENT to have if you plan to do a lot of Indian cooking. As coconut palms are grown in coastal areas, coconut milk naturally features in dishes from the western, southern and eastern parts of India.

Coconut milk is derived from squeezing freshly grated coconut flesh to extract all the flavour and juice. The resulting liquid is quite different from the thin coconut water found inside the coconut. Make sure the coconut flesh is white, as any sign of yellow indicates the fruit is becoming rancid and should not be used.

Since the process of splitting the coconut and grating it is quite tedious, you can use the canned variety sold in most Asian grocery shops and some supermarkets. But for the connoisseur, there certainly is a difference between freshly squeezed coconut milk and canned. Unfortunately, the freshly squeezed milk doesn't have any keeping qualities and has to be used quite quickly. This recipe explains how to make thick and thin coconut milk, both of which are used in recipes throughout this book. In most Indian cooking, the thin coconut milk is used first and then the thicker milk is added later in the recipe to impart a creamy, sweet flavour.

MAKES ABOUT 150 ML/5 FL OZ/⅔ CUP EACH OF THICK AND THIN
COCONUT MILK
freshly grated flesh of 1 coconut
150 ml/5 fl oz/⅔ cup warm water

SOAK THE GRATED COCONUT with 100 ml/4 fl oz/½ cup of the water for 15 minutes. Press through a fine sieve/strainer or squeeze in muslin/cheesecloth. Reserve this liquid to use as thick coconut milk.

Soak the residue with the remaining warm water for 15 minutes, then strain or squeeze again. Reserve this liquid to use as thin coconut milk.

DAHI Ⓥ
Natural Yogurt

YOGURT IS MILK which has been intentionally coagulated by a bacterial culture, and the great thing about it is that it retains all the nutritional components that make up milk. No whey is drained and no protein is separated.

Yogurt features a great deal in the Indian cuisine. It is served as a savoury accompaniment to meals, called *raita* (page 126), on its own with meals, or watered down to make the drinks *lassi* (page 56) and *chaas* (page 57). In cooking, yogurt is one of the basic ingredients in *Achar Gosh*t (page 141), or a souring agent in a host of other dishes. Parsis and Bengalis particularly enjoy it sweetened as a dessert.

MAKES ABOUT 1.2 LITRES/2 PINTS/5 CUPS
1.2 litres/2 pints/5 cups whole milk
4 tablespoons natural set whole-milk yogurt

BRING THE MILK to the boil, then remove it from the heat and leave it to cool until it is 46°–50°C/118°–125°F. Whisk in the yogurt with a wire whisk, then leave to set, uncovered, in a warm place for 6–8 hours until the yogurt looks set; do not stir. Transfer to the refrigerator, where it will keep for up to 2 days.

PANCH PHORAN Ⓥ
Five Whole Spices For Tempering
SEE PHOTOGRAPH ON PAGE 31

'TEMPERING' in Indian cooking means adding a spice or a herb, or a combination, to hot oil at the beginning or end of cooking to produce a unique flavour. It grows on you the more often you are exposed to it. Bengali chefs, and those from the states of Uttar Pardesh and Bihar, often use this technique. Some West Bengal chefs prefer to include a spice called *randhuni*, with a flavour similar to celery, but it is very difficult to get hold of outside Bengal.

For the perfect flavour, this combination of spices should be rinsed, drained and then laid out on kitchen paper/paper towels left to be sun-dried. But in the case that the sun refuses to come out from behind the clouds, leave the spices in a low oven to dry.

MAKES ABOUT 10 TABLESPOONS
4 tablespoons cumin seeds, rinsed and dried
3 tablespoons brown mustard seeds, rinsed and dried
2 tablespoons fennel seeds, rinsed and dried
1 tablespoon onion seeds, rinsed and dried
2 teaspoons fenugreek seeds, rinsed and dried

KEEP ALL THE SPICES in an airtight container for up to 6 months. Make sure they are completely dry or they will develop mildew and won't keep as long.

USING TAMARIND

TAMARIND, OR *IMLI*, is a bean-like fruit that is very sour in its raw state. In cooking it is used as a souring agent and to impart colour. Lemon juice is a substitute, albeit not a very good one. When tamarind pulp is cooked with spices and tempered it is excellent as a dip and in chutneys, such as the one on page 44.

Tamarind is sold ripe in Asian food shops, usually in compressed blocks which must be soaked before being used. To do this, soak each 450 g/1 lb tamarind pulp in 600 ml/1 pint/2½ cups water at room temperature for 2 hours until soft.

Press the softened pulp through a fine sieve/strainer, a little at a time. Remember to scrape off all the thick mixture on the bottom of the sieve. The pulp that is left inside the sieve can be soaked again with 300 ml/½ pint/1¼ cups water and then strained to extract the maximum amount of pulp.

In this state, the tamarind will keep in a covered container in the refrigerator for up to one week. For longer storage, bring the strained pulp to the boil, then simmer for 5 minutes, stirring occasionally. Allow to come to room temperature, then refrigerate in an airtight jar for up to four weeks.

Papadoms
on Fresh Mint

Starters and Drinks

NOWHERE WILL YOU SEE Bombay's kaleidoscope of cuisines and cultures more clearly than in the array of starters, appetizers and snacks served in homes, in restaurants, from stalls and on street corners. A South Indian family might sit down to an *idli* – a little rice-and-*dal* cake – which has been steamed, or a *medu vada* – a dumpling similar to a savoury doughnut. A family from Gujerat, however, might stave off their pangs of hunger an hour before dinner with a *poha*, which is a dish of savoury flaked rice, or maybe even a *vada pao* – a potato dumpling served in a bread roll. A Maharashtran family, on the other hand, might start their Sunday lunch with a few fried vegetables or fresh prawns/shrimp.

Starters, appetizers, snacks – the distinctions get blurred around the edges in Bombay. Many of our starters, or appetizers, at the Brasserie are drawn from the dazzling snack culture of Bombay's streets. Snacking is part of every Bombayite's day. An office worker might pop out for a quick bite as early as 10 o'clock – maybe he'll grab the ever-popular Bombay stand-by, a chutney sandwich, spread with green coconut chutney and filled with tomatoes and cucumber. Or instead he might head over to a South Indian *udipi* restaurant, traditionally run by the Shetty families, to snack on a *dosa*, a deliciously crisp pancake/crêpe made from rice and *dal* batter, served with spicy potatoes and onions and a tangy chutney.

At sundown, office workers and their families pack Chowpatty – the beachfront at the Bombay Opera House and Juhu – strolling, relaxing, taking in the air and, inevitably, snacking. As the sun sinks and the lights go on in the skyscrapers on Nariman Point across the bay, families cluster around the snack stalls that have become a Bombay culinary institution. Perhaps they will have a *gol gappa* – a puffed out, flaky, bite-size puri bread, which the vendor fills with a mixture of potatoes, chick-peas, chillies and onions, adds a spoonful of very spicy tamarind water and passes to a waiting hand to be popped into a waiting mouth for an instant explosion of flavour.

Once the stalls were known as *thelas*, meaning pushcarts, but nowadays they are often permanent, licensed sites, locked up at night and opened again in the morning. The stalls themselves are very picturesque with a nice big mound of *sev* – crisp vermicelli made from chick-pea flour – as a centrepiece. (It's a wonder sometimes how they take anything off without the whole collapsing.) Around this the vendor marshalls a neat array of ingredients, including small crispy puris, boiled potatoes which are cut at lightening speed, sprouted lentils, chutneys of chilli, tamarind and mint, extra sauces, sweetened yogurt and freshly ground cumin. It's up to you to pick and mix, take your tailor-made snack, and savour the flavours as the evening sky turns from orange to purple across the Indian Ocean.

SOUPS

THE IDEA OF SOUP as a separate course was a British invention in India. But if you delve into the ancient realms of Indian culinary heritage, soups and broths have always been a part of domestic meals – often in the form of a thin sauce, usually to be poured over rice. In northern India, soup might be called a *shorba* and enriched with yogurt; in the south, made from lentils and flavoured with tamarind, it's a *rasam*. But the British demanded their soup course, so a Madras *rasam* of lentil stock spiced up with pepper became Mulligatawny, literally 'pepper water' from the Tamil *milagu* (pepper) and *tunni* (water). It became one of the most famous culinary staples of the Raj.

More elaborate soups were prepared by the cooks catering to the Moghul emperors. These *shorbas* took the essence of their flavour from the *yakhni*, or marrow stock, flavoured with whole spices from all over Asia.

Soups are popular in India today, some eaten before the meal, some with the meal to moisten the rice. It's in the colder months that you'd expect to find soups on household menus. When I say cold, of course, these things are relative: in Bombay, people start shivering when the mercury drops below 20°C/66F°.

MULLIGATAWNY Ⓥ
Mulligatawny
SEE PHOTOGRAPH ON PAGE 47

FOREVER ASSOCIATED WITH THE RAJ, and possibly the best-known soup out of India, the name simply means 'pepper water'. It is made with a spiced lentil stock and spiked with black peppercorns. In Europe, Mrs Beeton and even L'Escoffier produced recipes for this. The combination of spices became so popular that many southern dishes repeat it in paste form.

SERVES 4
65 g/2½ oz/ ½ cup yellow lentils, well rinsed
65 g/2½ oz/½ cup red lentils, well rinsed
1 red apple, quartered
20 black peppercorns   6 curry leaves, optional
3 cloves
2 sprigs fresh coriander/cilantro leaves
2.5 cm/1 inch piece of cinnamon stick
1 cm/½ inch piece of fresh root ginger, peeled
2 teaspoons turmeric
1 teaspoon coriander seeds   ½ teaspoon cumin seeds
½ teaspoon Kashmiri red chilli powder or cayenne pepper
¼ teaspoon fenugreek seeds
salt, to taste
freshly crushed black peppercorns, to taste
lemon juice, to taste
boiled rice and chopped fresh coriander/cilantro leaves, to garnish

PLACE ALL THE INGREDIENTS, except the salt, crushed peppercorns and lemon juice, into a large saucepan and bring to the boil. Continue boiling until the lentils are tender. Strain and press the mixture through a fine sieve/strainer, discarding anything left behind in the sieve. Add enough water to the soup to make a pouring consistency. Bring to the boil and season with salt, crushed peppercorns and lemon juice. The seasoning should be quite sharp with a peppery bite. Serve garnished with a few grains of boiled rice and chopped coriander/cilantro.

TAMATAR KA SHORBA Ⓥ
Tomato Soup

THE SEASON FOR TOMATOES varies from region to region in India because it is such a large sub-continent. This is a very typical Hydrabadi recipe: a thin tomato broth, tempered with garlic. It would be served hot and traditionally drunk from a glass, rather than in a bowl to be eaten with a spoon.

SERVES 4
900 g/2 lb ripe tomatoes, halved
6 fresh mint leaves   4 cloves
3 garlic cloves, crushed   2 whole green chillies
2 sprigs fresh coriander/cilantro
2 bay leaves
1 large potato, peeled and sliced
1 cm/½ inch piece of fresh root ginger, peeled and sliced
½ teaspoon Kashmiri red chilli powder or cayenne pepper
¼ teaspoon turmeric
pinch of brown sugar   salt, to taste
chopped fresh coriander/cilantro leaves, to garnish

FOR THE TEMPERING
2 teaspoons vegetable oil
1 garlic clove, sliced   ¼ teaspoon ajwain seeds

PLACE ALL THE INGREDIENTS, except the ones for tempering, in a large saucepan and bring to the simmer, stirring. Continue simmering over a low heat until the tomatoes become very soft and the potato is mushy. Add 450 ml/16 fl oz/2 cups water to help soften the potato because the tomatoes have enough liquid on their own. Strain and press the soup through a fine sieve/strainer. Add salt.

To temper, heat the oil in a small ladle over a low flame, then add the garlic slices and ajwain. Pour this over the soup. Re-heat the soup and serve, garnished with the chopped coriander/cilantro leaves.

DAL SHORBA ⓥ
Yellow Lentil Soup

THIS IS A SIMPLE, light purée of flavoured yellow lentils. At the Bombay Brasserie it is a favourite with younger guests, including toddlers, and popular with vegetarians because it is an excellent source of vegetable protein.

SERVES 4

1 tablespoon vegetable oil

½ teaspoon cumin seeds

½ onion, sliced

65 g/2 ½ oz/½ cup yellow lentils, well rinsed and soaked for 15 minutes

50 g/2 oz/½ cup fresh coconut, grated

1 cm/½ inch piece of fresh root ginger, peeled

1 cm/½ inch piece of cinnamon stick

4 green cardamom pods   4 black peppercorns

3 cloves

2 sprigs fresh coriander/cilantro

1 teaspoon turmeric   ½ teaspoon cumin seeds

½ teaspoon Kashmiri red chilli powder or cayenne pepper

1 teaspoon lemon juice

salt, to taste

chopped fresh coriander/cilantro leaves, to garnish

HEAT THE OIL in a large saucepan. Add the cumin seeds and stir until they begin to crackle. Stir in the onion and continue frying, stirring occasionally, until they turn light brown. Add the remaining ingredients, except the lemon juice and salt, and stir-fry for about 2 minutes.

Stir in 750 ml/1¼ pints/3 cups water and simmer for about 40 minutes until the lentils are tender and have absorbed all the water. You may have to add a little extra water depending on the intensity of the heat. Strain and press the soup through a fine sieve/strainer. Re-heat the soup and season with the lemon juice and salt. Serve garnished with chopped coriander/cilantro leaves.

TAMATAR RASAM ⓥ
Tomato and Lentil Soup

A TYPICAL SOUTH INDIAN SOUP: there are many kinds of *rasams*; but this one is a light, spiced lentil soup. The cooked lentils are not puréed, but left to settle down in the soup, which is then decanted by ladle. A good *rasam* should be nice and tingly – you should feel it in the back of your throat. If you have a bunged-up nose, it should clear it!

SERVES 4

2 tablespoons red lentils, well rinsed

6 black peppercorns

2 large tomatoes, cubed

2 green chillies, slit or whole, as desired

1 sprig fresh coriander/cilantro

0.5 cm/¼ inch piece of fresh root ginger, peeled

1 tablespoon tamarind pulp (page 33)

2 teaspoons Kashmiri red chilli powder or cayenne pepper

1 teaspoon turmeric

salt, to taste

FOR THE TEMPERING

½ tablespoon vegetable oil

6 curry leaves

5 fenugreek seeds

¼ teaspoon brown mustard seeds

pinch of ground asafoetida

PUT THE LENTILS and remaining ingredients, except those for the tempering, in a large saucepan and and bring to the boil, then lower the heat and simmer for 20 minutes.

To temper, heat the oil in a ladle over a low flame. Add the curry leaves, fenugreek and mustard seeds and asafoetida and continue heating until the seeds crackle. Pour over the soup and stir in. Let the soup stand for a minute so the lentils settle, then ladle, steaming hot, into bowls.

MARG
Lamb Broth

A WARMING SOUP for the cold North Indian winters. This lamb, or mutton, broth – thinner than a *shorba* – is quite a classic and special soup. It's a Moghlai and Hydrabadi combination; a favouite of Moghuls from central Northern India. Since this soup is strained before finishing, it is economical to use lamb bones without meat on them. Throw in a couple of pieces of meat that you can chop just before serving.

SERVES 6

*900 g/2 lb mutton or lamb thigh and shank bones, including a few pieces of
meat to be chopped later*

225 ml/8 fl oz/1 cup natural yogurt (page 33)

4 tomatoes, diced

2 onions, sliced

1 garlic clove, sliced

1 cm/½ inch piece of fresh root ginger, peeled and sliced

4 sprigs fresh coriander/cilantro

2 sprigs fresh mint

6 green chillies

6 cloves

6 green cardamom pods   3 black cardamom pods

1 tablespoon coriander seeds

1 tablespoon turmeric

1 teaspoon cumin seeds

2 tablespoons vegetable oil

2 tablespoons gram flour

salt, to taste

PLACE ALL THE INGREDIENTS, except the oil, gram flour and salt, into a large saucepan. Add 5 litres/8¾ pints/5½ quarts water and slowly bring to the boil, uncovered. Lower the heat and simmer for about 2 hours. The stock should reduce considerably – add extra water if it looks as if there won't be enough. Strain and press the soup through a fine sieve/strainer, reserving a few pieces of lamb to use as a garnish.

Heat the oil for tempering in a small pan. Add the gram flour and stir until it bubbles and turns golden. Pour this over the strained soup. Do this very carefully as the flour tends to splash. Whisk in the flour, then return the soup to a slow simmer.

Add salt to taste. Serve garnished with finely chopped meaty lamb pieces.

JEHANGIRI SHORBA
Moghlai Chicken Soup

VERY MUCH LIKE A *MARG* (page 39), but made with chicken. A classic Moghlai recipe, supposedly a favourite of the great Moghul Emperor Jehangir. The recipe I learned was made with a chicken carcass and the aroma intrigued me even before I tasted it. A butcher will be happy to give you the fresh chicken carcasses.

SERVES 6

5 chicken carcasses, well rinsed and crushed

3 tablespoons vegetable oil

2 onions, sliced

4 tomatoes, diced

225 ml/8 fl oz/1 cup natural yogurt (page 33)

2.5 cm/1 inch piece of fresh root ginger, peeled and sliced

10 whole garlic cloves

6 green chillies

4 sprigs fresh coriander/cilantro

1 sprig fresh mint

1 tablespoon ground coriander

1 tablespoon garam masala (page 28)

1 tablespoon turmeric

2 teaspoons Kashmiri red chilli powder or cayenne pepper

1 teaspoon ground cumin

salt, to taste

FOR THE TEMPERING

1 tablespoon vegetable oil

1 tablespoon gram flour

1 teaspoon cumin seeds

1 garlic clove, peeled and sliced

BRING A LARGE PAN of water to the boil and add the chicken bones, then drain well. Heat the oil in a large stockpot or saucepan. Add the onion and fry until browned. Add the remaining ingredients, except the bones, and fry, stirring constantly, for about 15 minutes. Add the chicken bones and continue frying for a further 10–12 minutes, stirring and breaking up the bones. Add 5 litres/8¾ pints/5½ quarts water and slowly bring to the boil. Lower the heat and simmer, uncovered, for 1 hour.

Heat the oil for tempering in a small pan. Add the gram flour, cumin seeds and garlic and fry until the flour turns brown. Pour this over the simmering stock, being very careful as the flour tends to splash and bubble. Strain the soup through a fine sieve/strainer. Return the soup to the boil and season to taste with the salt. Serve steaming hot, garnished with chopped coriander/cilantro leaves.

SEAFOOD STARTERS

BOMBAY STARTED LIFE as a fishing village of the Koli fishing people, and the boats still go out. As it's a wealthy town, it doesn't need to export its catch, so the pick of the nets goes to the city's restaurants and domestic tables. One starter Bombay is famous for, of course, is Bombay Duck. It's actually a small fish otherwise known as *bombloe*, caught in the waters around Bombay and dried in the sun – a powerful aroma. Served crispy-fried, this traditional delicacy goes back to Bombay's earliest days, and was much admired by the first British settlers in the seventeenth century – so much so that they acquired the nickname 'Ducks' themselves.

MALABARI KEKRA
Crab Malabari

CRAB MEAT is uniquely sweet on its own, with the particularly sweet white meat coming mainly from the claws. The brown meat, which can have a distinctive fish flavour, on the other hand, comes from the body. For this dish, use all white meat. It is sold fresh and vacuum packed from fishmongers and large supermarkets.

SERVES 4

4 teaspoons vegetable oil
½ teaspoon brown mustard seeds
8 curry leaves, chopped, optional
1 onion, chopped
2 tomatoes, peeled and chopped
2 teaspoons ground coriander
1½ teaspoons Kashmiri red chilli powder or cayenne pepper
1 teaspoon turmeric
450 g/1 lb fresh flaked white crab meat with any bits of shell removed
50 g/2 oz/½ cup fresh coconut, grated
2 teaspoons tamarind pulp (page 33)
salt, to taste
chopped fresh coriander/cilantro leaves, to garnish

HEAT THE OIL in a small saucepan. Add the mustard seeds and curry leaves and stir until they crackle. Add the onions and sauté for 2–3 minutes, then stir in the tomatoes and continue cooking for a further minute. Stir in the coriander, chilli powder and turmeric and continue stirring for 2 minutes. Add the crab meat, turn up the heat and stir-fry for a couple of minutes until the aroma starts wafting up. Stir in the coconut, tamarind pulp and salt. Serve hot, garnished with chopped coriander/cilantro leaves.

SHRIMP MASALA
Tiny Shrimp Cooked in Goan Masala

THIS IS A VERY POPULAR DISH on the restaurant menu. It is best eaten in small quantities with Indian bread. Naans are excellent (page 69), but plain bread rolls will suffice.

SERVES 4

450 g/1 lb raw small shelled shrimp, thawed if frozen

1 tablespoon lemon juice

1 teaspoon Kashmiri red chilli powder or cayenne pepper

½ teaspoon turmeric

salt, to taste

2 tablespoons vegetable oil

5 garlic cloves, sliced   1 large onion, chopped

3 tomatoes, chopped

2 tablespoons dark rum

FOR THE RED MASALA

12–14 dried red chillies, or 1½ tablespoons Kashmiri red chilli powder or

cayenne pepper

8 black peppercorns

5 cloves

4 green cardamom pods   4 garlic cloves

2.5 cm/1 inch piece of cinnamon stick

2.5 cm/1 inch piece of fresh root ginger, peeled

¼ nutmeg, grated

3 tablespoons malt vinegar

TO MAKE THE MASALA, place the chillies, peppercorns, cloves, cardamom pods, garlic, cinnamon, ginger and nutmeg in an electric spice mill and blend until a fine powder forms. Add the vinegar a little at a time so the masala is smooth; set aside. Place the shrimp in a glass bowl. Add the lemon juice, chilli powder, turmeric and salt and leave to marinate for 15–20 minutes. Heat the oil in a saucepan. Add the shrimp and stir-fry for 3–4 minutes until they turn pink. Remove the shrimp with a slotted spoon; set aside.

Add the garlic to the pan and stir-fry until the aroma of cooked garlic is evident. Add the onion and continue stir-frying until almost brown, then add the tomatoes and continue cooking for 3–4 minutes. Add the rum and masala and continue stir-frying for a further 3–4 minutes until the fat separates. Return the shrimp to the pan and stir all the ingredients together. Continue stir-frying for 1–2 minutes, but no longer or the shrimp will be too firm. Add salt to taste. Serve at once with lots of bread.

MAHI TIKKA
Fish Tikka

HERE'S HOW TO COOK FISH to succulent perfection using yogurt and light spicing. The marinade is very much in the tadoori style, but the fish is actually cooked in a conventional oven. Be sparing with the ajwain, however, as this is strongly flavoured and can easily overpower the fish. Cod is ideal, but monkfish makes the dish more special.

SERVES 4

900 g/2 lb cod fillets, skinned, boned and cut into 2.5 cm/1 inch cubes
2 tablespoons lemon juice
salt, to taste
2 tablespoons vegetable oil
100 ml/4 fl oz/½ cup natural yogurt (page 33)
1 tablespoon Kashmiri red chilli powder or cayenne pepper
1 teaspoon Mace, Nutmeg and Green Cardamom powder (page 29)
1 teaspoon ajwain seeds
1 teaspoon mustard powder
1 teaspoon ground white pepper
½ teaspoon turmeric
salt, to taste
1 onion, sliced, to garnish
1 lemon, cut into wedges, to garnish

PLACE THE FISH CUBES in a glass bowl. Add the lemon juice and salt and leave to marinate for 2 hours. Combine the remaining ingredients in another bowl and whisk together. Pour over the fish; leave at room temperature for 1 hour.

Arrange the fish in a single layer in a large ovenproof dish and bake in an oven preheated to 190°C/375°F/Gas 5 for 18–20 minutes until the fish flakes easily when tested with the tip of a knife.

Serve straight from the oven, garnished with onion slices and lemon wedges.

TANDOORI SCALLOPS
Scallops Baked in a Tandoori Masala
SEE PHOTOGRAPH ON PAGE 46

SCALLOPS are not a well-known type of seafood in India, but keeping in mind their exotic appearance and flavour, I developed this recipe using a tandoori marinade.

SERVES 4

15 cashew nuts
12 large scallops on the half shell
juice of ½ lemon   salt, to taste
225 ml/8 fl oz/1 cup natural yogurt (page 33)
2 teaspoons Kashmiri red chilli powder or cayenne pepper
1 teaspoon Mace, Nutmeg and Green Cardamom powder (page 29)
1 teaspoon turmeric
½ teaspoon ground white pepper
1 tablespoon vegetable oil
12 fresh coriander/cilantro leaves, to garnish

SOAK THE CASHEW NUTS in 350 ml/12 fl oz/1½ cups warm water for about 30 minutes. Place the nuts and liquid in an electric spice mill and grind until a smooth paste forms; set aside. Meanwhile, rinse the scallops in the shell and pat dry with kitchen paper/paper towels. Sprinkle with lemon juice and salt; set aside. Place all the remaining ingredients, except the coriander/cilantro leaves, in a bowl and whisk together. Place the coriander leaves in a bowl of cold water to keep fresh and crisp.

Spoon an equal amount of the mixture over each scallop's white flesh; do not cover the roe because it looks naturally attractive. Arrange the scallop shells in a single layer in a shallow baking tray and cook in an oven preheated to 220°C/425°F/Gas 7 for 4 minutes. Lower the temperature to 190°C/375°F/Gas 5 and cook for a further 4–5 minutes. Test one scallop to make sure it is cooked through; cut it in half and it should be uniformly white and not translucent. Serve at once, each scallop garnished with a coriander leaf.

JHINGA PATTICE
Shrimp Patties with a Medley of Chutneys

PATTICES ARE FAVOURITES of Bombayites in restaurants and at food stalls. On the road-side stalls, you will see a large cast-iron griddle with sizzling potato cakes, which are the *pattices*, and a selection of chutneys – hot as well as sweet and sour – and accompaniments, such as chick-peas, onions, fresh coriander/cilantro and ground masalas. This *pattice*, however, is a bit more adventurous, with the potato cakes stuffed with a spicy shrimp masala and served with three colourful chutneys.

The selection of chutneys here can also be used in a whole range of *chaats* and kababs. I think it is most convenient to keep small airtight jars of the tamarind chutney and chilli chutney in the refrigerator, ready to use. They keep for about two weeks.

If you have them on hand, you can make the *pattice* with instant mashed potatoes so the preparation of the dish is quick, but I still prefer freshly boiled potatoes for their natural taste.

SERVES 4

3 large potatoes

salt, to taste

2 tablespoons vegetable oil

1 small onion, chopped

2 teaspoons Ginger and Garlic Paste (page 29)

100 g/4 oz small raw shelled shrimp, thawed if frozen

2 teaspoons Kashmiri red chilli powder or cayenne pepper

1 teaspoon turmeric

1 teaspoon ground coriander

1 teaspoon garam masala (page 28)

2 sprigs fresh coriander/cilantro leaves, chopped

1 teaspoon lemon juice

salt, to taste

1 tablespoon vegetable oil

flour for dusting

extra coriander/cilantro, to garnish

FOR TEMPERING THE POTATOES

2 teaspoons vegetable oil

6 curry leaves, chopped, optional

1 green chilli, chopped

0.5 cm/¼ inch piece of fresh root ginger, peeled and chopped

½ teaspoon cumin seeds

½ teaspoon turmeric

¼ teaspoon ground asafoetida

FOR THE TAMARIND CHUTNEY

225 g/8 oz jaggery or dark brown sugar

100 g/4 oz tamarind

6 ripe dates, stoned/pitted

0.5 cm/¼ inch piece of fresh root ginger, peeled and chopped

1 tablespoon sugar   2 teaspoons black salt

1 teaspoon Kashmiri red chilli powder or cayenne pepper

1 teaspoon dried ground ginger

2 teaspoons vegetable oil   ½ teaspoon cumin seeds

salt, to taste

FOR THE MINT AND YOGURT CHUTNEY

SEE PHOTOGRAPHS ON PAGES 66 AND 104

3 sprigs fresh mint leaves, chopped

3 sprigs fresh coriander/cilantro leaves, chopped

1 cm/½ inch piece of peeled fresh root ginger, chopped

2 green chillies   ¼ teaspoon cumin seeds

225 ml/8 fl oz/1 cup natural yogurt (page 33)

salt, to taste

FOR THE CHILLI CHUTNEY

125 g/4½ oz/½ cup tomato ketchup

1 tablespoon malt vinegar   2 teaspoons vegetable oil

2 teaspoons Kashmiri red chilli powder or cayenne pepper

1 teaspoon Ginger and Garlic Paste (page 29)

TO MAKE THE TAMARIND CHUTNEY, place the jaggery, tamarind, dates, fresh ginger, sugar, black salt, chilli powder and ground ginger in a large saucepan. Add 4.3 litres/2½ pints/1½ quarts water and slowly bring to the boil, stirring, then lower the heat and simmer for 30 minutes. Pour the hot mixture through a fine sieve/strainer; take care not to touch it because it is like caramel and will burn you. Heat the oil in a small ladle. Remove from the heat, add the cumin seeds and then pour over the strained chutney. Add salt. Leave to cool.

Meanwhile, boil the unpeeled potatoes until they are tender. Drain and peel them when they are cool enough to handle, then mash. For the tempering, heat the oil in a small frying pan/skillet. Add all the tempering ingredients and fry for a minute until the aroma starts wafting up. Pour over the mashed potatoes, add salt and stir together; set aside. Heat 1 tablespoon of the oil in a saucepan. Add the onion and fry until crisp and golden brown. Add the ginger and garlic paste and fry until the aroma of cooked garlic is evident. Stir in the shrimp, chilli powder, turmeric and ground coriander and stir-fry for 4–5 minutes. Sprinkle with the garam masala, coriander/ cilantro, lemon juice and salt. The mixture should not be too runny or it will make the *pattices* soggy; any excess oil can be drained off and reserved to use in other seafood dishes.

To shape the *pattices*, form the mixture into 4 balls. Flatten each slightly and make an indentation in the centre with a tea-spoon. Fill with a little of the shrimp mixture and re-form the pattice to completely enclose the shrimp mixture. Dust lightly with flour.

Heat the remaining 1 tablespoon vegetable oil in a large frying pan/skillet until medium-hot. Add the *pattices* and fry until they are golden brown on both sides, frying in batches if necessary. Drain well on crumpled kitchen paper/paper towels. Keep warm in an oven preheated to 150°C/300°F/Gas 2 until you are ready to serve.

To make the mint and yogurt chutney, place all the ingredients, except the yogurt and salt, in a blender and blend until a fine paste forms, adding 50–100 ml/2–4 fl oz/¼–½ cup water. Whisk this paste together with the yogurt and salt in a glass bowl. Cover and chill until required. To make the chilli chutney, mix all the ingredients together in a glass bowl. The mint and yogurt and chilli chutneys are not cooked chutneys.

Place one *pattice* on a plate and spoon the chutneys around it to give a colourful appearance for serving. Serve garnished with the coriander/cilantro.

PATRANI MACCHI
Fish with Mint Chutney in Banana Leaves

SEE PHOTOGRAPH ON PAGE 46

THIS IS A PARSI FAVOURITE – you would be served this in a Parsi home or at a large wedding feast. The banana leaves impart a unique flavour, but if they aren't available kitchen foil works just as well, retaining all the wonderful aromas and flavours of the ingredients. Instead of using string to tie up the parcels, sometimes I shred the leaf vein and use it like a string. Thai and some Chinese food shops sell banana leaves.

The chutney in this recipe is best smoothly ground in a stone pestle, but the next best gadget to use is an electric blender.

SERVES 4

2 medium pomfret, sole or plaice, filleted and skinned
juice of 1 lemon   salt, to taste
2 teaspoons turmeric
4 banana leaves, 20 × 20 cm/8 × 8 inches

FOR THE MINT CHUTNEY
grated flesh of 1 small fresh coconut, or 100 g/4 oz/1 cup dessicated/shredded
coconut
20 sprigs fresh coriander/cilantro

12 sprigs fresh mint leaves
4 green chillies
4 garlic cloves
1 cm/½ inch piece of fresh root ginger, peeled and chopped
2 tablespoons distilled white vinegar
1 tablespoon vegetable oil
2 teaspoons turmeric
1 teaspoon sugar
salt, to taste

PLACE THE FISH FILLETS in a glass bowl. Add the lemon juice, salt and turmeric and gently mix together; set aside. Place all the ingredients for the chutney is a stone mortar or a blender and process until a thick, smooth paste forms. Add a little water if necessary.

Coat the fish pieces liberally with the green chutney. Place each piece on a banana leaf and wrap the leaf around the fish to enclose it completely. Tie each parcel securely with a string. Steam the parcels for 18–20 minutes. Or, arrange in a shallow baking tray with 100 ml/4 fl oz/½ cup water and cook in an oven preheated to 190°C/375°F/Gas 5 for 25–30 minutes.

Serve hot with the leaf still wrapped around the fish. Diners then discard the leaf as they eat the fish.

PREVIOUS SPREAD, clockwise from bottom left: Tossed Salad (*page 56*); Lassi (*page 57*); Tandoori Scallops (*page 43*); pomfret; Mulligatawny Soup (*page 37*); Naan (*page 69*); Patrani Macchi (*page 48*).

NON-VEGETARIAN STARTERS

A RANGE OF MEAT DISHES are consumed as accompaniments with pre-dinner drinks here at the Brasserie. These include fried kababs or tandoori kababs. In Bombay as well, you will find these sold on every street corner and in restaurants.

In addition to the two recipes in this section, you can serve any of the chicken *tikka* recipes in the tandoori chapter (pages 62–4) with drinks or as a first course. These recipes have always been popular on the Bombay Brasserie menu.

SHAMMI KABABS
Spiced Lamb Patties

THESE ARE SHALLOW FRIED PATTIES of minced/ground lamb, yellow split gram – you'll see it sold as *channa dal* in Asian grocery shops – and herbs and spices. The mixture is cooked and shaped in advance and fried just before serving.

MAKES 8

1 tablespoon vegetable oil, plus 4 tablespoons for frying
450 g/1 lb minced/ground lamb, not too lean
100 g/4 oz/½ cup split yellow gram or channa dal
2.5 cm/1 inch piece of cinnamon stick
1 cm/½ inch piece of fresh root ginger, peeled and chopped
10 black peppercorns   6 green cardamom pods
5 garlic cloves
5 dried red chillies, or 2 teaspoons Kashmiri red chilli powder or cayenne
pepper
4 green chillies   3 black cardamom pods
2 cloves
3 sprigs fresh coriander/cilantro leaves
1 sprig fresh mint leaves
cornflour/cornstarch for dusting
Mint and Yogurt Chutney (page 44), to serve
onion slices, to garnish

HEAT 1 TABLESPOON OIL in a large saucepan until it reaches the smoking point. Add all the remaining ingredients, except the extra oil, cornflour/cornstarch, chutney and onion slices. Stir rapidly to sear the lamb. After about 1 minute, the lamb will become a bit watery. Lower the heat and simmer, covered, for about 50 minutes, stirring frequently, until the lamb is very tender.

Remove the mixture from the pan and set aside to cool. Pass it though a meat mincer/grinder or process it in a food processor. Place in a sieve/strainer over the sink and leave until all the fat has drained away.

Knead the drained mixture with your hands and shape into 8 balls. Flatten each ball slightly and dust with cornflour to prevent them breaking up during frying.

Heat the remaining oil in a large frying pan. Add the meat patties and fry them on both sides, in batches if necessary, until they are brown and crisp on the outsides. Drain well on crumpled kitchen paper/paper towels.

Serve hot with a mint and yogurt dip chutney and onion slices.

SEEKH KABABS
Minced/Ground Lamb on a Skewer

IN MUSLIM *DARGAS*, or mosque areas, like Mahim in Bombay, you'll find vendors' stalls in the evening laden with 40–50 kg/100–125 lb of mince/ground meat, and the vendors busy skewering and cooking *sheek kababs* and naans. At the Brasserie we use whole pieces of lamb minced with the herbs and spices.

The secret of a good *seekh kabab* is to use prime meat, not trimmings – we mince a whole boned leg! The trick to get the mince to stay on the skewer is to dip your hand in water and rub it along the skewer before you add the meat – I promise you the meat will then stay in position. These also cook perfectly on a barbecue.

SERVES 4

450 g/1 lb leg of lamb, minced/ground with the fat included

4 garlic cloves, finely chopped

3 green chillies, finely chopped

3 sprigs fresh coriander/cilantro leaves, finely chopped

1 sprig fresh mint leaves, chopped

1 onion, chopped

0.5 cm/¼ inch piece of fresh root ginger, peeled and chopped

15 g/½ oz/1 tablespoon chilled butter, diced

2 teaspoons Kashmiri red chilli powder or cayenne pepper

2 teaspoons garam masala (page 28)

1 teaspoon turmeric

salt, to taste

sliced onions and lemon wedges, to garnish

Mint and Yogurt Chutney (page 44), to serve

MIX ALL THE INGREDIENTS TOGETHER, then finely chop or mince/grind in a meat mincer or mince in a food processor for 2 minutes. Transfer to a glass bowl, cover and chill for at least 20 minutes. Mould 2 plump sausages on to each of 4 long metal skewers. The ideal way to cook these is on a barbecue over smouldering charcoal. If you don't have a barbecue, however, preheat the oven to 220°C/425°F/Gas 7 and heat a few pieces of charcoal under a hot grill/broiler until they start smouldering. Use tongs to place them in the bottom of a deep baking tray. Suspend the skewers across the top of the tray and cook the kababs for 8–10 minutes, turning the skewers occasionally, until cooked through. Serve hot, garnished with the onions and lemon and with the yogurt and mint chutney.

VEGETARIAN STARTERS

IN BOMBAY, the population is almost equally divided between vegetarians and non-vegetarians, and at the Brasserie we have always made sure there are plenty of meatless snacks and starters/appetizers on the menu. These are a few of the most popular.

DAHI PAKODI Ⓥ
Fried Dumplings with Yogurt and Chutneys

THESE ARE GRAM FLOUR DUMPLINGS and as well as being a delicious vegetarian first course, they can also be served as an accompaniment to main courses, such as you would serve a *raita*.

MAKES 20 PIECES

65 g/2½ oz/½ cup black lentils or urad dal, well rinsed and drained
300 g/10 oz/2 cups gram flour
150 g/5 oz/1 cup self-raising/self-rising flour
3 fresh green chillies, finely chopped
1 cm/½ inch piece of fresh root ginger, peeled and finely chopped
1 tablespoon seedless raisins
pinch of baking powder
salt, to taste
vegetable oil for deep-frying
2 tablespoons Tamarind Chutney (page 44), to serve
2 tablespoons Chilli Chutney (page 44), to serve
chopped fresh coriander/cilantro leaves, to garnish

FOR THE SWEETENED YOGURT

450 ml/16 fl oz/2 cups natural yogurt (page 33)
1½ teaspoons sugar
1 teaspoon ground cumin
½ teaspoon black salt
salt, to taste

LEAVE THE LENTILS to soak in water to cover for 1 hour. Transfer to a blender or food processor, add the gram flour and self-raising/self-rising flour and blend until a smooth paste forms, adding a little water if necessary. The paste should be of dropping consistency. Transfer the paste to a bowl and stir in the chillies, ginger, raisins, baking powder and salt. Mix together, then set aside for 15–20 minutes. To make the sweetened yogurt, place all the ingredients in a large glass bowl and whisk with a wire whisk. Check the seasoning, which should be on the sweet side. Cover and chill until ready to serve.

To fry the dumplings, heat the oil in a *kadai* or wok until it is 180°C/350°F, or until a cube of bread will brown in about 45 seconds. Drop in medium-size balls of the lentil and flour mixture and fry until golden brown all over, working in batches. Drain well on crumpled kitchen paper/paper towels and leave for 5 minutes. Transfer the dumplings to a bowl of warm water, large enough that they are all covered with water, and leave for 8–10 minutes. Use your hands to remove the dumplings from the water and squeeze dry, then immerse them in the bowl of sweetened yogurt. Spoon on to side plates and top with a dash of the yogurt and the chutneys. Serve garnished with coriander/cilantro.

RAGARA PATTICE Ⓥ
Potato Cakes with Spiced Chick-Peas

A CLASSIC EXAMPLE of Bombay roadside fare. There you will see stalls with a big griddle with spicy chick-peas on one side, already cooked with chillies, and *pattices*, or potato patties, on the other side. You can make the spiced chick-peas in advance and re-heat them when you are ready to serve. If you use canned chick-peas, however, be careful with the seasoning because many are canned in brine.

SERVES 4

2 tablespoons yellow split gram or channa dal

1 teaspoon Kashmiri red chilli powder or cayenne pepper

salt, to taste

2 large potatoes

2 tablespoons vegetable oil

6 curry leaves, optional

1 green chilli, finely chopped

0.5 cm/¼ inch piece of fresh root ginger, peeled and finely chopped

1 teaspoon shop-bought chaat masala

½ teaspoon turmeric

2 tablespoons Mint and Yogurt Chutney (page 44), to serve

2 tablespoons Tamarind Chutney (page 44), to serve

2 tablespoons Chilli Chutney (page 44), to serve

chopped fresh coriander/cilantro, to garnish

FOR THE SPICED CHICK-PEAS

200 g/7 oz/1 cup dried chick-peas

1 tablespoon vegetable oil

1 onion, chopped

2 teaspoons Ginger and Garlic Paste (page 29)

100 ml/4 fl oz/½ cup natural yogurt (page 33)

2 teaspoons ground coriander

1 teaspoon Kashmiri red chilli powder or cayenne pepper

1 teaspoon turmeric

½ teaspoon ground cumin

1 tomato, finely chopped

1 green chilli, finely chopped

salt, to taste

1 teaspoon garam masala (page 28)

TO PREPARE THE CHICK-PEAS, soak them in water to cover for 6 hours. Drain the chick-peas well, re-cover with fresh water and bring to the boil, then lower the heat and simmer for 35–40 minutes until soft. Drain well. Heat the oil in a saucepan. Add the onion and fry until light brown, stirring occasionally. Add the ginger and garlic paste and stir-fry for about 1 minute until the aroma of cooked garlic is evident. Use a fork to mix the yogurt with the ground coriander, chilli powder, turmeric and ground cumin. Gradually stir this into the pan and cook, stirring rapidly, for about 3 minutes. Stir in the chick-peas and 100 ml/4 fl oz/½ cup water and simmer for

about 2 minutes. Add the tomato, chilli and salt and sprinkle with garam masala. Bring to the boil, then turn off the heat. Set aside and keep warm until ready to serve, or leave to cool completely and re-heat when required.

To make the *pattices*, place the yellow split gram in a saucepan with water to cover and bring to the boil. Lower the heat and simmer for 30 minutes until the gram are tender. Drain and stir in chilli powder and salt. Meanwhile, boil the potatoes until tender. Drain and peel when they are cool enough to handle, then mash.

Heat ½ tablespoon of the oil in a large frying pan/skillet. Add the curry leaves, green chilli, ginger, chaat masala and turmeric and fry for 1 minute, stirring occasionally. Add the mashed potatoes, turn off the heat and stir until all the ingredients are well blended. Transfer to a bowl and leave until cool enough to handle.

Use your hands to shape into 4 large balls or 8 smaller ones. Flatten each slightly and make an indentation in the centre. Add the softened yellow gram and completely cover with the spiced mashed potatoes. Flatten into a patty about 7.5 cm/3 inches across.

Heat the remaining 1½ tablespoons oil in a large frying pan/skillet. Add one or two *pattices* at a time and fry until crisp and golden brown on both sides. Drain well on crumpled kitchen paper/paper towels.

To assemble, place each *pattice*, or 2 if you have made smaller ones, in the centre of a plate and use the palm of your hand to flatten. Spread the chick-peas on top at the 12 o'clock position, put the mint and yogurt chutney at the 3 o'clock position, the tamarind chutney at the 6 o'clock position and the chilli chutney in the 9 o'clock position. Sprinkle chopped coriander/cilantro over the chick-peas and serve.

ALOO TUK Ⓥ
Fried Potatoes with Sweet Yogurt

A VERY SINDHI ITEM, from the area in the far North-West of India. There cooks fry their potatoes with skin until crisp and then sprinkle them with a selection of ground masalas. Here at the Bombay Brasserie, we've taken the Sindhi concept and coverted into a *chaat*, using hot fried potatoes with yogurt and chutneys on top. The result is hot and crisp, yet cooling at the same time.

SERVES 4

20 small new potatoes, well scrubbed
vegetable oil for deep-frying
2 teaspoons Kashmiri red chilli powder or cayenne pepper, plus extra to garnish
2 teaspoons ground cumin, plus extra to garnish
1 teaspoon ground black salt, plus extra to garnish
salt, to taste
1 quantity Sweetened Yogurt (page 155), to serve
2 tablespoons Tamarind Chutney (page 44), to serve
chopped fresh coriander/cilantro leaves, to garnish

BOIL THE POTATOES in their skins until they are very tender, then drain well. When cool enough to handle, smash and flatten each between your palms. Heat enough oil to deep-fry the potatoes in a *kadai* or wok. Add the potatoes, in batches, and fry until the skins are crisp and golden brown. Remove the potatoes with a slotted spoon and transfer to a colander over the sink to drain.

Toss the potatoes with the chilli powder, ground cumin, black salt and salt. Equally divide the potatoes between individual plates and put a dollop of sweetened yogurt on top of each. Add some tamarind chutney. Sprinkle with extra chilli powder, ground cumin, black salt and coriander/cilantro leaves for garnish.

SAMOSA CHAAT Ⓥ
Potatoes in Crisp Fried Pastry

CHAAT MEANS, literally, a spicy or tangy snack. In this recipe the samosa pastry, which has been filled with a savoury mixture, is made into a *chaat* by the addition of sweetened yogurt and a selection of chutneys.

SERVES 4

2 large potatoes

1 tablespoon vegetable oil

1 tablespoon shop-bought chaat masala

2 teaspoons dried mango powder

1 teaspoon Kashmiri red chilli powder or cayenne pepper

1 teaspoon ground coriander

1 teaspoon turmeric

½ teaspoon ground cumin

65 g/2½ oz/½ cup shelled green peas

salt, to taste

crushed black pepper, to taste

vegetable oil for deep-frying

1 quantity Spiced Chick-Peas (page 52), to serve

1 quantity Sweetened Yogurt (page 155), to serve

2 tablespoons Tamarind Chutney (page 44), to serve

2 tablespoons Chilli Chutney (page 44), to serve

chopped fresh coriander/cilantro leaves, to garnish

shop-bought chaat masala and ground cumin, to garnish

FOR THE SAMOSA PASTRY/DOUGH

300 g/10 oz/2 cups plain/all-purpose flour

½ teaspoon caraway seeds

salt, to taste

15 g/½ oz/1 tablespoon ghee or clarified butter, melted

TO MAKE THE PASTRY/DOUGH, sift the flour into a bowl, add the caraway seeds and salt and stir together. Make a well in the centre and pour in the ghee, then rub it in with your fingertips until a crumbly mixture forms, very much like making Western shortcrust pastry/piecrust dough. Add water sparingly and knead until a firm pastry forms. Cover with a warm, wet towel and leave to rest for at least 20 minutes.

Meanwhile, boil the potatoes until just tender. Drain and peel when cool enough to handle, then cut into small cubes. To prepare the filling, heat the oil in a *kaдai* or wok. Add the chaat masala, dried mango powder, chilli powder, ground coriander, turmeric and ground cumin. Stir-fry for 1 minute, then add the potatoes and peas and stir until well combined, breaking and mashing the potatoes as you stir. Simmer for about 5 minutes, then add salt and pepper. Remove from the heat and leave to cool. Roll out the pastry on a lightly floured surface, flipping and dusting it occasionally, until it is 2–3 mm/¹⁄₁₆–⅛ inch thick. Cut it into four 14 cm/5¾ inch squares, then cut each square diagonally in half to make 8 triangles.

To assemble a samosa, wet the longest side of one of the pastry triangles with a finger dipped in water. Shape it into a cone and use water to seal the edges. Put the potato filling into the cone. Wet the open edges with water and fold over to form a sealed pyramid. Heat the oil in a deep-fat fryer or large saucepan until 150°–160°C/300°–325°F, or a cube of bread browns in about 60 seconds. Working in batches, deep-fry the samosas for about 12 minutes until golden brown. Transfer to crumpled kitchen paper/paper towels to drain. To serve, divide the chick-peas between the individual plates and add 2 hot samosas. Ladle some sweetened yogurt on top, and add the chutneys. Garnish with chopped coriander/cilantro and a pinch of ground cumin and chaat masala.

SALAD STARTERS

SALAD MAY NOT be immediately associated with Indian cuisine, but these days almost every household table includes one, even if it is just salted sliced tomatoes. And it may not always be a raw salad – the ingredients may be cooked very quickly in hot oil and mustard seeds for extra flavour.

CURRIMBHOY SALAD Ⓥ
Currimbhoy Salad

THIS IS A TYPICAL SALAD from the Taj repertoire, created many years ago for one of our regular guests. If you are surprised to see mayonnaise in an Indian recipe, remember that previous generations of Indian cooks were heavily influenced not just by British but also by Continental cuisine. Continental cooking skills are particularly associated with a sect of cooks with the surname Gomes. Originally from Bengal, they converted to Christianity from Hinduism, and are synonymous with the catering industry in India. This salad is equally good as a main course accompaniment. I like it with fried snacks and kababs.

SERVES 4

1 large head Iceberg lettuce, well rinsed, drained and leaves cut into
1 cm/½ inch cubes
3 hard-boiled eggs, shelled and roughly chopped
2 garlic cloves, finely chopped
1 small pickled gherkin, finely chopped
1 small onion, finely chopped
1 green chilli, finely chopped
3 tablespoons shop-bought low-fat mayonnaise
½ teaspoon freshly ground black pepper
salt, to taste, if required
4 sprigs fresh coriander/cilantro, to garnish

PLACE THE CHOPPED LETTUCE in a large bowl. Add all the remaining ingredients and lightly mix together. Cover and chill for at least 5 minutes before serving. Serve garnished with coriander/cilantro.

TOSSED SALAD
Tossed Salad

SEE PHOTOGRAPH ON PAGE 46

AS IMPLIED BY THE TITLE, the ingredients are simply thrown together. What is interesting, however, is that this combination is a slimmer's delight, but a double portion provides a satisfying, balanced meal; the paneer provides the protein and the vegetables provide lots of other nutrients. This is always popular with our figure-conscious clients.

SERVES 4

1 head Iceberg or Cos/Romaine lettuce, well rinsed and drained
1 small red pepper, cored, seeded and diced
1 small green pepper, cored, seeded and diced
1 small yellow pepper, cored, seeded and diced
1 yellow grapefruit, peeled, segmented and diced
5 cm/2 inch piece of paneer, grated, to ganish

FOR THE DRESSING
2 tablespoons sunflower oil   1 tablespoon lemon juice
1 teaspoon chopped fresh coriander/cilantro leaves
½ teaspoon ground pepper   ½ teaspoon sugar
¼ teaspoon mustard powder
salt, to taste

QUARTER THE LETTUCE and remove and reserve the large outer leaves. Dice the remaining inner leaves. Place the lettuce and remaining salad ingredients, except the paneer, in a bowl, toss together and chill for at least 30 minutes. Place all the ingredients for the dressing in a glass bowl and whisk together to form a suspension. To serve, place the reserved large leaves in the bottom of a glass bowl. Toss the salad ingredients with the dressing and arrange on top of the lettuce leaves. Sprinkle the grated paneer over the top and serve at once.

DRINKS

LASSI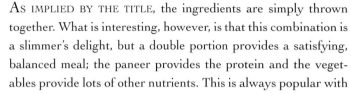
Yogurt Drink

SEE PHOTOGRAPH ON PAGE 46

THIS IS THE MOST WIDELY CONSUMED BEVERAGE in India, with everyone in northern India drinking it almost daily. In southern India, however, it is thinner and tempered with curry leaves and mustard seeds, while in Bengal it is sweetened and called *ghol*. And in Bombay, of course, you will find all the variations readily available. Both variations here should be made with home-made yogurt, but shop-bought natural set yogurt is equally satisfying. Use ice cubes to chill your drink or make in a big jug and chill in the refrigerator before serving.

MEETHA LASSI ⓥ
Sweet Yogurt Drink

MAKES 5 GLASSES

1.2 litres/2 pints/5 cups natural yogurt (page 33)

2 tablespoons sugar

pinch of salt

pinch of ground cumin

PUT THE YOGURT, sugar and salt in a large jug with 300 ml/ 10 fl oz/1¼ cups water and whisk until frothy. Pour into glasses and serve sprinkled with the ground cumin.

KHARA LASSI ⓥ
Salted Yogurt Drink

MAKES 5 GLASSES

1.2 litres/2 pints/5 cups natural yogurt (page 33)

¾ teaspoon salt

½ teaspoon sugar

pinch of ground cumin

Put the yogurt, salt and sugar in a large jug with 300 ml/ 10 fl oz/1¼ cups water and whisk until frothy. Pour into glasses and serve sprinkled with the ground cumin.

CHAAS ⓥ
Light Yogurt Drink

CHAAS is a watered down version of the *lassi* – almost like whey but still containing all the goodness of whole milk yogurt. It is light and an excellent accompaniment throughout the whole meal.

MAKES 4 GLASSES

600 ml/1 pint/2½ cups natural yogurt (page 33)

salt, to taste

1 teaspoon chopped fresh coriander/cilantro leaves

1 teaspoon chopped peeled fresh root ginger

½ teaspoon finely chopped green chilli

½ teaspoon ground cumin

1 teaspoon vegetable oil (optional)

PUT THE YOGURT and salt in a large jug with 600 ml/1 pint/2½ cups water and whisk until frothy.

Pour into glasses and sprinkle over the coriander/cilantro leaves, ginger, chilli and cumin. If you want a more aromatic version, fry the coriander, ginger, chilli and cumin in 1 teaspoon oil in a ladle, then sprinkle over the tops.

JAL JEERA ⓥ
Cumin Water

A VERY COOLING AND REFRESHING DRINK for hot weather, rather like sipping Pimms while watching a cricket match in the sun. I can assure you from experience it is an excellent aperitif, and really does get the gastric juices flowing. Black salt is easily available from Indian food stores. If you can't find any, however, just omit it and don't be tempted to substitute ordinary table salt.

MAKES 4 SMALL GLASSES

1 tablespoon cumin seeds   1 teaspoon black salt

1 teaspoon shop-bought chaat masala

1 teaspoon tamarind pulp (page 33)

1 teaspoon chopped fresh coriander/cilantro leaves

½ teaspoon chopped fresh mint leaves

pinch of sugar   lemon slices, to garnish

SOAK THE CUMIN SEEDS in 600 ml/1 pint/2½ cups water for 6 hours. Strain and reserve the liquid; the seeds can be thoroughly dried and used again. Add the remaining ingredients to the water and stir together well. Cover and chill for at least an hour. When ready to serve, stir well and garnish each glass with a lemon slice.

Bitter Gourd
and Arbi on Chilli Powder

Tandoori Specialities

Tandoor simply means 'oven' – traditionally a clay shell, fired in early days with wood and now with charcoal. Tandoori cuisine is almost exclusively North Indian. The first tandoor ovens were for communal use, set into the ground in a communal area of the village. In the evening, the women would take their kneaded dough down to the tandoor and sit and gossip around it while they took turns flattening the dough and popping it in. The light, thin breads that resulted would be wrapped in cloth and taken home for the family. Nowadays, larger or more affluent households might have their own set-in tandoor out in the back garden.

Tandoori cooking started with breads; but it developed as an ideal way of cooking meats and even vegetables, on long metal skewers stood inside the tandoor. The meat had to be moist and well-cooked at the same time – in India you won't see people eating meat rare. Yogurt was a natural choice to moisten the meat, flavoured with a whole range of spices – cardamoms, cloves, bay leaves, chilli, peppercorns. The recipes for these masalas, or combinations of spices, in which the meat was marinaded overnight, became an art form, a jealously guarded secret. At North Indian banquets, cooks would vie with each other to create more and more exotic tandoori dishes – a huge joint here, a whole goat there, all in the chef's special tandoori masala.

The tandoor grills and bakes at the same time. Unlike a barbecue, the moisture given off by the food is retained inside the shell. With the lid of the tandoor shut, the result is both dry heat from the charcoal, and steam from the food, creating a pressure-cooker effect. The skewer also rests in the red-hot charcoal, transferring the heat right to the inside of the food. The result, if handled properly, is meat that is meltingly tender yet throroughly cooked, beautifully spiced by the masala with the lingering hint of charcoal.

It's healthy, too. Tandooris call for good-quality meats, with all excess fat trimmed to leave a nice marbling. With chicken, the leg joints are actually more suited to tandoori cooking than the breast, which can be a little dry. Fish can be tandooried, but it needs to be cooked whole, skewered from head to tail. Contrary to popular belief, it is possible to tandoori at home. One solution is to try it on a garden barbecue, especially if you have one of those barbecues with a hemispherical sealing lid. This, to some extent, copies the behaviour of a tandoor by retaining the moisture given off by the food. Alternatively, you can cook these recipes in the oven, although you should allow air to circulate around the food in some way – using skewers, a rotisserie or even a wire tray – and not just sit it in a roasting tray to stew in the marinade.

But it is also possible to turn your domestic oven into a real charcoal tandoor – I've tried this, and it works! First, a word on safety: your kitchen must be very well ventilated. If you can, open all the windows and close the kitchen door while you cook, or else the cooker must be fitted with an efficient extractor hood that's ducted through to the outdoors.

First, marinate the food as instructed in the recipe. It's better to use smaller cuts of meat, or, if it's a chicken, joint it and remove the bones. This is a *tandoori tikka*, where *tikka* means, literally, a cut of meat rather than the whole bird. Skewer it on metal skewers. Take a deep roasting tray and cover the bottom with about ten pieces of normal barbecue charcoal. (You need a tray that's deep enough for you to rest the skewered food across it and still have a 2-inch clearance above the charcoal.) Light the charcoal or heat it under the grill so that it smoulders. Rest the skewers across the tray and put it into a hot oven – 240°C/475°F/gas 9. Keep the oven door a little open, because the moment the marinade starts dripping, you'll have smoke. Using this method, friends of mine have achieved results that compare very favourably with a real tandoori oven.

TANDOORI MURGH
Marinated Roast Chicken

IF YOU ARE one of those lucky persons with a huge oven and a rotisserie you can roast the chickens whole. Otherwise, joint each bird into two legs and two breasts. You can also barbecue the whole birds or joints.

SERVES 4

2 chickens, each about 1 kg/2¼ lb, skinned and jointed if necessary (see Introduction)

juice of 1 lemon

salt, to taste

sliced onions and lemon wedges, to garnish

Mint and Yogurt Chutney (page 44), to serve

FOR THE TANDOORI MARINADE

750 ml/1¼ pints/3 cups natural yogurt (page 33)

2 tablepsoons vegetable oil

1 tablespoon Ginger and Garlic Paste (page 29)

1 tablespoon Kashmiri red chilli powder or cayenne pepper

2 teaspoons ground coriander

2 teaspoon garam masala (page 28)

2 teaspoons dry mustard powder

1 teaspoon turmeric

1 teaspoon ground white pepper

MAKE GASHES DIAGONALLY ACROSS the grain of the flesh of the chickens. Rub with lemon juice and salt and set aside for 10 minutes. Meanwhile, to make the marinade, place the yogurt in a glass bowl and whisk in the remaining ingredients and salt to form a smooth paste. Add the chicken pieces and make sure they are well coated, then leave to marinate for 6 hours at room temperature or for 12 hours in the refrigerator.

When ready to cook, preheat the oven to 230°C/450°F/Gas 8 and heat a few pieces of charcoal under a hot grill/broiler until they start smouldering. Use tongs to place them in the bottom of a deep baking tray. Skewer the chicken pieces on long metal skewers and suspend them across the top of the tray. Roast the chicken until the juices stop dripping, which should take about 15 minutes. Transfer the skewers to a hot grill and grill until the chicken pieces look chargrilled. Serve hot, garnished with the onions and lemons and with the yogurt and mint chutney.

HARIALI CHICKEN TIKKA
Marinated Chicken with Yogurt and Green Herbs

SEE PHOTOGRAPH ON PAGE 66

FROM THE PUNJAB, 'the green land', where when they harvest chefs use lots of green herbs in the cooking. The greenness in this recipe comes from the spinach, coriander/cilantro, mint, peppers and green chillies. This can be cooked equally well on a barbecue.

SERVES 4

2 chickens, each about 1 kg/2¼ lb, skinned, boned and cut into 24 pieces

juice of 1 lemon

salt, to taste

4 whole green chillies

1 large green pepper, cored, seeded and coarsely chopped

½ bunch fresh spinach leaves, well rinsed and shaken dry

½ bunch fresh coriander/cilantro leaves, chopped

½ bunch fresh mint leaves, chopped

1 tablespoon Ginger and Garlic Paste (page 29)

1 tablespoon tamarind pulp (page 33)

2 teaspoons garam masala (page 28)

¼ teaspoon turmeric

450 ml/16 fl oz/2 cups natural yogurt (page 33)

1 tablespoon vegetable oil

2 teaspoons ground white pepper

sliced onions and lemon wedges, to garnish

Mint and Yogurt Chutney (page 44), to serve

RUB THE CHICKEN PIECES with lemon juice and salt and set aside for 10 minutes. Meanwhile, place the chillies, green pepper, spinach, coriander/cilantro, mint, ginger and garlic paste, tamarind pulp, garam masala and turmeric in a blender or food processor and blend until a smooth paste forms. Transfer the paste to a large glass bowl and beat in the yogurt, oil, pepper and salt. Add the chicken pieces and make sure they are well coated, then leave to marinate for 4 hours at room temperature or for 8 hours in the refrigerator. When ready to cook, preheat the oven to 230°C/450°F/Gas 8 and heat a few pieces of charcoal under a hot grill/broiler until

they start smouldering. Use tongs to place them in the bottom of a deep baking tray.

Skewer the chicken pieces on long metal skewers and suspend them across the top of the tray. Roast the chicken for 18–20 minutes until cooked through and the juices run clear when tested with the tip of a knife. Transfer the skewers to a hot grill and grill until the chicken pieces look chargrilled.

Serve hot garnished with the onions and lemons and with the yogurt and mint chutney.

MURGH TIKKA
Boneless Chicken with a Tandoori Marinade
SEE PHOTOGRAPH ON PAGE 66

THE WORD *TIKKA* literally means 'a cut', so in this recipe the bird is boned and cut into pieces before it is marinated. This is an ideal way to serve chargrill chicken as a snack with cocktails, or as part of a finger buffet. If you are adventurous, vary the ingredients in the marinade. This can be cooked equally well on a barbecue.

SERVES 4

2 chickens, each about 1 kg/2¼ lb, skinned, boned and cut into 24 pieces
juice of 1 lemon
salt, to taste
1 quantity Tandoori Marinade (page 61)
sliced onions and lemon wedges, to garnish
Mint and Yogurt Chutney (page 44), to serve

RUB THE CHICKEN PIECES with lemon juice and salt and set aside for 10 minutes. Meanwhile, prepare the marinade in a large glass bowl. Add the chicken pieces and make sure they are well coated, then leave to marinate for 4 hours at room temperature or for 8 hours in the refrigerator.

When ready to cook, preheat the oven to 230°C/450°F/Gas 8 and heat a few pieces of charcoal under a hot grill/broiler until they start smouldering. Use tongs to place them in the bottom of a deep baking tray. Skewer the chicken pieces on long metal skewers and suspend them across the top of the tray. Roast the chicken for 18–20 minutes until cooked through and the juices run clear when tested with the tip of a knife. Transfer the skewers to a hot grill and grill until the chicken pieces look chargrilled. Serve hot, garnished with the onions and lemons and with the yogurt and mint chutney.

MALAI MURGH TIKKA
Roast Marinated Chicken with Yogurt and Cheese
SEE PHOTOGRAPH ON PAGE 66

MALAI MEANS CREAM – this marinade uses yogurt and cream for a creamy consistency. It's very mild, but with the the mace, nutmeg and green cardamom powder it's also very aromatic. This recipe is also good cooked on a barbecue.

SERVES 4

2 chickens, each about 1 kg/2¼ lb, skinned, boned and cut into 24 pieces
juice of 1 lemon
2 teaspoons crushed peppercorns   salt, to taste
450 ml/16 fl oz/2 cups natural yogurt (page 33)
2 tablespoons double/heavy cream
2 tablespoons grated mild cheese, such as Cheddar
1 tablespoon Ginger and Garlic Paste (page 29)
1 tablespoon vegetable oil   2 teaspoons ground white pepper
1½ teaspoons Mace, Nutmeg and Green Cardamom powder (page 29)
sliced onions and lemon wedges, to garnish
Mint and Yogurt Chutney (page 44), to serve

RUB THE CHICKEN PIECES with lemon juice, pepper and salt and set aside for 10 minutes. Meanwhile, place the yogurt in a large glass bowl and whisk in the cream, cheese, ginger and garlic paste, vegetable oil, white pepper, the mace, nutmeg and cardamom powder and salt. Add the chicken pieces and make sure they are well coated, then leave to marinate for 2 hours at room temperature or for 6 hours in the refrigerator. When ready to cook, preheat the oven to 230°C/450°F/Gas 8 and heat a few pieces of charcoal under a hot grill/broiler until they start smouldering. Use tongs to place them in the bottom of a deep baking tray. Skewer the chicken pieces on long metal skewers and suspend them across the top of the tray. Roast the chicken for 18–20 minutes until cooked through and the juices run clear when tested with the tip of a knife. Transfer the skewers to a hot grill and grill until the chicken pieces look chargrilled. Serve hot, garnished with the onions and lemons and with the yogurt and mint chutney.

ACHARI MURGH TIKKA
Marinated Chicken with Pickling Spices

SEE PHOTOGRAPH ON PAGE 66

ACHARI is the Indian word for 'pickling spices', which flavour the marinade. This recipe is equally delicious cooked on a barbecue.

SERVES 4

2 chickens, each about 1 kg/2¼ lb, skinned, boned and cut into 24 pieces

juice of 1 lemon

salt, to taste

1 tablespoon cumin seeds   1 tablespoon coriander seeds

2 teaspoons fennel seeds   2 teaspoons yellow mustard seeds

1 teaspoon fenugreek seeds   ½ teaspoon onion seeds

225 ml/8 fl oz/1 cup vegetable oil

100 ml/4 fl oz/½ cup malt or distilled vinegar

1 tablespoon jaggery or light brown sugar, dissolved in 225 ml/8 fl oz/

1 cup water

450 ml/16 fl oz/2 cups natural yogurt (page 33)

1 tablespoon Ginger and Garlic Paste (page 29)

2 teaspoons turmeric

2 teaspoons Kashmiri chilli powder or cayenne pepper

sliced onions and lemon wedges, to garnish

Mint and Yogurt Chutney (page 44), to serve

RUB THE CHICKEN PIECES with lemon juice and salt and set aside for 10 minutes. Meanwhile, dry-roast the cumin, coriander, fennel, mustard, fenugreek and onion seeds in a frying pan/skillet for 3–4 minutes until the aroma of roasted spices wafts up. Transfer to an electric spice mill or pestle and process until coarsely ground.

Heat the oil in a large saucepan and heat the vinegar and dissolved jaggery in another pan. Add the spices to the pan, then immediately start to slowly pour in the vinegar mixture; be very careful, as it tends to bubble and splash. Remove from the heat and leave to cool completely. Place the yogurt in a large glass bowl and whisk in the ginger and garlic paste, turmeric, chilli powder, salt and the cool spice mixture until a smooth marinade forms. Add the chicken pieces and make sure they are well coated, then leave to marinate for 4 hours at room temperature or for 12 hours in the refrigerator.

When ready to cook, preheat the oven to 230°C/450°F/Gas 8 and heat a few pieces of charcoal under a hot grill/broiler until they start smouldering. Use tongs to place them in the bottom of a deep baking tray. Skewer the chicken pieces on long metal skewers and suspend them across the top of the tray. Roast the chicken for 18–20 minutes until cooked through and the juices run clear when tested with the tip of a knife. Transfer the skewers to a hot grill and grill until the chicken pieces look chargrilled. Serve hot, garnished with the onions and lemons and with the yogurt and mint chutney.

TANDOORI TROUT
Roast Marinated Trout

SEE PHOTOGRAPH ON PAGE 66

YOU CAN COOK ANY FISH this way, provided they are not too large – say less than 450 g/1 lb in weight each. They should be gutted but still left on the bones, and of a size that will fit in your oven. Threading a skewer though a whole trout may take a bit of practice. If you mess it up, however, don't worry. Just cook the pieces in a baking tray basted with the marinade – the results will be different, but still delicious.

SERVES 4

12 cashew nuts
4 trout, each about 400 g/14 oz, scaled, gutted through the belly and
well rinsed
juice of 1 lemon
salt, to taste
450 ml/16 fl oz/2 cups natural yogurt (page 33)
1 tablespoon Kashmiri red chilli powder or cayenne pepper
1 tablespoon vegetable oil
2 teaspoons Ginger and Garlic Paste (page 29)
2 teaspoons garam masala (page 28)
2 teaspoons turmeric
½ teaspoon ajwain seeds
sliced onions and lemon wedges, to garnish
Mint and Yogurt Chutney (page 44), to serve

SOAK THE CASHEW NUTS in water to just cover for about 30 minutes. Place the nuts and liquid in an electric blender and blend until a thick, smooth paste forms; set aside. Meanwhile, make diagonal slits on both sides of the trout. Place in a single layer in a glass dish and rub with lemon juice and salt and set aside for 10–15 minutes. To make the marinade, place the yogurt in a large glass bowl and whisk in the nut paste, chilli powder, vegetable oil, ginger and garlic paste, garam masala, turmeric, ajwain seeds and salt. Pour over the trout and make sure they are well coated, then leave to marinate for 2 hours at room temperature or for 4 hours in the refrigerator.

When ready to cook, preheat the oven to 230°C/450°F/Gas 8 and heat a few pieces of charcoal under a hot grill/broiler until they start smouldering. Use tongs to place them in the bottom of a deep baking tray. Skewer the trout on to long, medium-thick metal skewers, starting from the nostrils, along the spine and through the tail. Suspend the skewers across the top of the tray. Roast the fish for 18–20 minutes until cooked through and the flesh flakes easily when tested with the tip of a knife. Transfer the skewers to a hot grill and grill until the fish look chargrilled. Serve hot, garnished with the onions and lemons and with the yogurt and mint chutney.

ADRAKI GOSHT KI CHAMPEN
Lamb Chops with Ginger and Herbs

SEE PHOTOGRAPH ON PAGE 66

HERE'S A REAL BOMBAY BRASSERIE SPECIAL of thick lamb chops, oozing with juice. These are English chops, unusually trimmed of all fat, and cooked the Indian style. These are also very good cooked on a barbecue.

SERVES 4–6

15–16 cashew nuts

12 thick-cut lamb chops, trimmed of all fat and beaten lightly

1 tablespoon vegetable oil

2 teaspoons ground white pepper

salt, to taste

450 ml/16 fl oz/2 cups natural yogurt (page 33)

4 green chillies, finely chopped

1 tablespoon Ginger and Garlic Paste (page 29)

2 teaspoons Mace, Nutmeg and Cardamom Powder (page 29)

1 teaspoon ground ginger

SOAK THE CASHEW NUTS in water to just cover for about 30 minutes. Place the nuts and liquid in an electric blender and blend until a thick, smooth paste forms; set aside. Meanwhile, place the lamb chops in a single layer in a large glass dish. Rub with with the oil, pepper and salt and set aside for 10–15 minutes. To make the marinade, place the yogurt in a large glass bowl and whisk in the nut paste, chillies, ginger and garlic paste, the mace, nutmeg and cardamom powder, ground ginger and salt. Pour over the chops and make sure they are well coated, then leave to marinate for 6 hours at room temperature or for 12 hours in the refrigerator.

When ready to cook, preheat the oven to 220°C/425°F/Gas 7 and heat a few pieces of charcoal under a hot grill/broiler until they start smouldering. Use tongs to place them in the bottom of a deep baking tray. Skewer the chops on long metal skewers. Suspend the skewers across the top of the tray. Roast the chops for 18–20 minutes until cooked through and they are starting to brown. Transfer the skewers to a hot grill and grill until they look chargrilled. Serve hot, garnished with the onions and lemons and with the yogurt and mint chutney. Wrap the exposed parts of the bones in kitchen foil. It's delicious to pick up the chops with your fingers and eat them hot.

PREVIOUS SPREAD, clockwise from bottom left: Malai Murgh Tikka (*page 63*), Murgh Tikka (*page 63*), Achari Murgh Tikka (*page 64*) and Hariali Murgh Tikka (*page 62*) with Mint and Yogurt Chutney (*page 44*); Adraki Gosht Ki Champen (*page 68*); Tandoori Trout (*page 65*); natural yogurt; Roti (*page 71*); Laccha Paratha (*page 72*); Naan (*page 69*); Kheema Naan (*page 70*).

NAAN
Leavened White Bread

SEE PHOTOGRAPHS ON PAGES 47 AND 67

UNFORTUNATELY, it's impossible to cook a real, authentic naan without an authentic *tandoor*. The technique involves rolling out the proofed dough, opening the lid of the tandoor and literally sticking the bread to the wall of the oven. Nevertheless, even with a domestic oven, this recipe should give good results.

You can use half the dough to make basic naans one day, then use the remaining dough to make the stuffed naan recipes (pages 70–71) the next day. Just cover the dough with cling film/plastic wrap and refrigerate it overnight, then let it come to room temperature before you use it.

MAKES 14

900 g/2 lb/6 cups plain/all-purpose flour
1 tablespoon baking powder
1 teaspoon sugar   salt, to taste
1 egg, lightly beaten
300 ml/10 fl oz/1¼ cups milk, boiled and cooled to about 50°C/126°F
4 tablespoons vegetable oil   2 tablespoons sesame seeds
melted butter for brushing, optional

SIFT THE FLOUR into a large bowl with the baking powder, sugar and salt and make a well in the centre. Add the egg, milk and 300 ml/10 fl oz/1¼ cups lukewarm water in small quantities, kneading with your fingers and adding more liquid as needed to make a very firm and tight dough. Cover the bowl with a warm, wet towel and leave to rise for 30 minutes. Punch down the dough. Add the oil and knead until it is thoroughly incorporated. Cover and leave to rise again for 1 hour. Punch down the dough and divide it into 14 equal balls. Place them on a tray dusted with extra flour, cover with a warm, wet towel and leave to rise for 30 minutes.

Roll out each dough ball on a lightly floured surface until it is about 0.5 cm/¼ inch thick and sprinkle with sesame seeds. (An experienced chef in the Brasserie kitchen would beat out the dough with his hands, but at home it is just as easy to roll it out.) Place the naans on a greased and heated baking sheet. Bake in an oven preheated to 240°C/475°F/Gas 9 for 5–6 minutes until golden brown and puffed up. Brush with melted butter before serving, if you like. Serve at once, while still hot.

KHEEMA NAAN
Naans Stuffed with Minced Lamb

SEE PHOTOGRAPH ON PAGE 67

AGAIN, this recipe uses half the basic Naan dough (see page 69).
Serve these warm as a main course or as a snack.

MAKES 8

½ quantity basic Naan dough (page 69)
1 tablespoon sesame seeds
melted butter for brushing, optional

FOR THE FILLING

2 teaspoons vegetable oil
½ teaspoon cumin seeds
1 teaspoon Ginger and Garlic Paste (page 29)
1 teaspoon ground cumin
1 teaspoon Kashmiri red chilli powder or cayenne pepper
½ teaspoon turmeric
225 g/8 oz lean minced/ground lamb
1 tablespoon chopped fresh coriander/cilantro leaves
½ teaspoon garam masala (page 28)
1 small potato, boiled, peeled and mashed
salt, to taste

SHAPE THE RISEN DOUGH into 8 equal balls. Place them on a tray dusted with extra flour, cover with a warm, wet towel and leave to rise for 15 minutes.

To make the filling, heat the oil in a saucepan. Add the cumin seeds and fry until they turn brown. Stir in the ginger and garlic paste and continue frying until the aroma of cooked garlic is evident. Add the ground cumin, chilli powder and turmeric and fry for a further minute. Add the lamb and stir-fry for 20–25 minutes until it is cooked through. Add a little water, if necessary to prevent the meat sticking, but the mixture should be dry.

Stir in the coriander/cilantro, garam masala, potato and salt and mix together well. Spoon the mixture into a fine wire sieve/strainer and leave over the sink so all the excess fat drains off as it cools; leave to cool completely. Flatten each dough ball, make a well in the centre and put an equal amount of filling in each. Re-shape into balls, completely enclosing the filling. Re-roll each ball until it is 0.5 cm/¼ inch thick. Sprinkle sesame seeds on top of each. Place the naans on a greased heated baking sheet and bake in an oven preheated to 220°–230°C/425°–450°F/Gas 7–8 for 8–10 minutes until golden brown. Brush with melted butter before serving, if you like. Serve at once, while still hot.

PANEER KULCHA
Naan Stuffed with Cottage Cheese

THIS USES the basic Naan dough and fills it with a spiced cheese mixture.

MAKES 8

½ quantity basic Naan dough (page 69)
1 tablespoon sesame seeds
1 teaspoon black onion seeds
1 tablespoon vegetable oil
melted butter for brushing, optional

FOR THE FILLING
100 g/4 oz paneer, grated
3 green chillies, finely chopped
0.5 cm/¼ inch piece of fresh root ginger, peeled and finely chopped
2 tablespoons chopped fresh coriander/cilantro leaves
1 tablespoon seedless raisins
1 teaspoon ground cumin
salt, to taste

SHAPE THE RISEN DOUGH into 8 equal balls. Place them on a tray dusted with extra flour, cover with a warm, wet towel and leave to rise for 15 minutes. Meanwhile, soak the sesame and onion seeds in the oil for 5 minutes. To make the filling, mix together the paneer, chillies, ginger, coriander/cilantro, raisins, ground cumin and salt.

Flatten each dough ball, make an indentation in the centre and put an equal amount of filling in each. Re-shape into balls, completely enclosing the filling. Re-roll each ball until it is 0.5 cm/¼ inch thick. Spread 1 teaspoon of the seed mixture over the top of each. Place the *kulchas* on a greased heated baking sheet and bake in an oven preheated to 220°–230°C/425°–450°F/Gas 7–8 for 8–10 minutes until golden brown. Brush with melted butter before serving, if you like. Serve at once, while still hot.

ROTI/CHAPATTI Ⓥ
Unleavened Wholemeal/Whole-Wheat Bread

SEE PHOTOGRAPHS ON PAGES 67 AND 113

JUST WHOLEMEAL/WHOLE-WHEAT FLOUR, salt and water. Cooked in a *tandoor* or the clay oven, this is a roti; cooked on a hot *tawa*, or a griddle, this is a chappati. In India it would be cooked on the side of a hot *tandoor* oven, but griddle or frying pan/skillet works just as well.

MAKES 6

450 g/1 lb/3 cups wholemeal/whole-wheat flour
salt, to taste

SIFT THE FLOUR into a bowl and add the salt. Add about 225 ml/ 8 fl oz/1 cup water, only a little at a time, and knead until a firm dough forms. Cover with a wet, warm towel and let rest for 20 minutes. Divide the dough into 8 equal portions and roll out on a lightly floured surface into thin rounds.

Preheat a *tawa* or frying pan/skillet until it is so hot that water sizzles instantly if a few drops are added. Cook one chapatti at a time until it brown, then flip it over to cook the other side. Remove and serve at once or keep warm. Continue until all the chappatis are cooked.

LACCHA PARATHA ⓥ
Layered Bread

SEE PHOTOGRAPHS ON PAGES 67 AND 113

Laccha means 'layered', and the word *paratha* indicates that a flour dough has been enriched with ghee or sometimes milk, as this one has. As you eat it, the layers will open out.

MAKES 6

75 g/3 oz/⅓ cup semolina

½ teaspoon saffron

225 ml/8 fl oz/1 cup milk

450 g/1 lb/3 cups plain/all-purpose, plus extra for dusting

½ teaspoon Mace, Nutmeg and Green Cardamom Powder (page 29)

salt, to taste

1 tablespoon vegetable oil

45 g/1½ oz/3 tablespoons ghee for brushing the bread, melted, plus extra for frying

PLACE THE SEMOLINA and saffron in the milk and set aside for 15 minutes. Sift the flour into a bowl and make a well in the centre. Pour in the saffron-flavoured milk and add the mace, nutmeg and cardamom powder and salt. Add about 175 ml/ 6 fl oz/¾ cup water, a little at a time, and knead until a firm dough forms. Make a well in the dough and knead in the oil, kneading for 10–15 minutes. Cover with a wet, warm towel, and let rest for 20 minutes. Divide the dough into 8 equal portions and leave to rest again for a further 20 minutes.

Roll out each dough ball on a lightly floured surface into the thinnest possible round. Brush each one with melted ghee and dust with flour. Working with one at a time, scrunch it up to form a long rope, then roll it up into a coil. Cover the rolls with a warm, wet towel and leave to rest for 20 minutes. Use a rolling pin and roll out the dough rolls on a lightly floured surface into a 15–17.5 cm/6–7 inch round. Melt the extra ghee in a *tawa* or frying pan/skillet over a low heat. Add one paratha at a time and cook, flipping over, until it is golden brown and crisp on both sides. Serve at once, and continue until all the parathas are cooked.

ALOO PARATHA ⓥ
Wholemeal/Whole-Wheat Bread Stuffed with Potatoes

THESE ARE BEST ENJOYED HOT as they come off the *tawa*, but you can keep them warm in a tightly covered casserole lined with a napkin for about 30 minutes.

MAKES 8

1 quantity Roti/Chapatti dough (page 71)

extra flour for dusting

vegetable oil or butter for frying

FOR THE FILLING

1 tablespoon vegetable oil

½ teaspoon cumin seeds

2–3 green chillies, finely chopped

0.5 cm/¼ inch piece of fresh root ginger, peeled and finely chopped

2 large potatoes, boiled, peeled and mashed

2 teaspoons shop-bought chaat masala

salt, to taste

2 tablespoons chopped fresh coriander/cilantro leaves

SHAPE THE DOUGH into 8 balls, then cover with a warm, wet towel and leave to rest while you prepare the filling. To make the filling, heat the oil in a frying pan/skillet. Add the cumin seeds and fry until they crackle. Add the chillies and ginger and continue frying until they brown lightly. Mix in the mashed potatoes, chaat masala and salt until well combined. Add the coriander/cilantro. Flatten each dough ball, make an indentation in the centre and put an equal amount of filling in each. Re-shape into balls, completely enclosing the filling. Re-roll each ball until it is 0.5 cm/¼ inch thick.

Preheat a *tawa* or frying pan/skillet until it is medium-hot. Add one paratha and cook it for about 50 seconds, then flip it over and cook for a further minute. Spoon over 1 tablespoon oil and continue cooking until it starts to fry, flipping the paratha over every 30 seconds until it is golden brown and crisp on both sides. Continue until all the parathas are cooked.

PUDINA PARATHA Ⓥ
Wholemeal/Whole-Wheat Bread with Fresh Mint

SEE PHOTOGRAPH ON PAGE 124

YOU CAN MAKE THIS BREAD either by kneading the mint into the dough, or by adding it in a mint chutney to layer the dough.

MAKES 8

METHOD 1	METHOD 2
450 g/1 lb/3 cups wholemeal/whole-wheat flour, plus extra for sprinkling	*450 g/1 lb/3 cups wholemeal/whole-wheat flour, plus extra for dusting*
¼ bunch fresh mint leaves, chopped	*1 tablespoon vegetable oil*
1 tablespoon vegetable oil	*salt, to taste*
salt, to taste	*25 g/1 oz/2 tablespoons ghee or butter, melted*
25 g/1 oz/2 tablespoons ghee or butter, melted	*2 tablespoons Green Masala Paste (page 98)*
	15 g/1 oz/1 tbsp vegetable oil
	vegetable oil for frying

METHOD 1

SIFT THE FLOUR into a bowl, adding any bran left behind in the sieve/sifter, and make a well in the centre. Add the mint, oil and salt and mix together. Add 175 ml/6 fl oz/¾ cup water, little by little, kneading until a firm dough forms. Cover the dough with a warm, wet towel and leave to rest for 15 minutes. Shape the dough into 8 balls. Roll out each dough ball on a lightly floured surface with a lightly floured rolling pin into a 20 cm/8 inch round. Brush each one with melted ghee and dust with flour. Working with one at a time, scrunch it up to form a long rope, then roll it up into a coil. (Unlike the dough for the Layered Bread (page 72) this dough does not need to be left to rise again.)

Roll out into a 15 cm/6 inch round about 0.5 cm/¼ inch thick on a lightly floured surface. Heat a *tawa* or frying pan/skillet until it is medium-hot. Add one paratha and cook it for about 50 seconds, then flip it over and cook for a further 30 seconds. Spoon over 1 teaspoon ghee and continue cooking until it starts to fry, flipping it over every 30 seconds until it is golden brown and crisp on both sides. Continue until all the parathas are cooked.

METHOD 2

SIFT THE FLOUR into a bowl, adding any bran left behind in the sieve/sifter, and make a well in the centre. Add the oil and salt and mix together. Add about 175 ml/6 fl oz/¾ cup water, little by little, kneading until a firm dough forms. Cover the dough with a warm, wet towel and leave to rest for 15 minutes. Shape the dough into 8 balls. Roll out each dough ball on a lightly floured surface with a lightly floured rolling pin into a 20 cm/ 8 inch round. Brush each one with melted ghee and green masala paste. Dust with flour. Working with one at a time, scrunch it up to form a long rope, then roll it up into a coil. (Unlike the dough for the Layered Bread (page 72) this dough does not need to be left to rise again.)

Roll out into a 15 cm/6 inch round about 0.5 cm/¼ inch thick on a lightly floured surface. Heat 1 tablespoon oil in a *tawa* or frying pan/skillet until it is medium-hot. Add one paratha and cook it for about 50 seconds, then flip it over and cook for a further 30 seconds. Spoon over 1 teaspoon oil and continue cooking until it starts to fry, flipping it over every 30 seconds until it is golden brown and crisp on both sides. Continue until all the parathas are cooked.

Aubergines
and Turmeric Root
on Turmeric Powder

Parsi Fare

THE PARSIS CAME ORIGINALLY FROM PERSIA and were instrumental in building Bombay – the Bombay Brasserie itself has strong Parsi connections (see Introduction). The great Parsi families of the city were both wealthy and powerful, and dined accordingly. Many adopted Western styles of eating using tablecloths, napkins and knives and forks and kept several chefs capable of preparing both European and Parsi dishes. Even today, you would be extremely grateful to receive an invitation to a Parsi wedding, or *laghan nu bhonu*: it's more like a Royal banquet, only served on banana leaves, with course after course, each one distinctly different from the last. Even the desserts might be six courses! At the banquet the distinctive Parsi non-alcoholic drinks are served, aerated and brightly-coloured, like *rooh afza*, a strawberry concoction.

The most orthodox Parsis used to have strict codes about how meals were taken. Only the fingers could be used, which were not allowed to touch any part of the mouth or lips for fear of becoming impure. Water had to be poured into the mouth without the glass touching the lips. Traditionally, Parsi men took their meals first, the women and children of the household eating after the men had finished. (But European manners became much stronger among wealthier Parsis and by the 1900s Parsi women could live a much more liberated existence than their Hindu counterparts.) The Parsi religion, while preaching temperance with alcohol, encourages its followers to eat well. The holy book, the *Vendidad*, formally rejects fasting and proclaims: 'He who eats not has no strength, whether to do valiant religious works, or to till the ground, or to beget vigorous offspring. It is by eating that the whole material world lives'.

Parsis are mostly meat eaters. Vegetables are included in meat dishes, but there are few solely vegetable dishes. The cuisine can be spicy, but it's rarely chilli-hot. The Persian influence of the ancient Parsi past remains in their cooking – in the use of dried fruits, for example. These recipes are typical Parsi fare – the kind of thing you'd find served at home, or as a course in a wedding banquet.

SALI BOTI
Sweet-and-Sour Lamb Curry with Straw Potatoes

SEE PHOTOGRAPH ON PAGE 85

DEEP-FRIED POTATO STRAWS are a traditional accompaniment to this dish. To prepare them, thinly slice three large peeled potatoes, then cut the slices into thin matchsticks. Sprinkle with salt. Heat enough vegetable oil for deep-frying in a deep saucepan until it is 180°C/350°F, or a cube of bread will brown in about 45 seconds. Add the potato matchsticks, in batches if necessary, and fry until light golden brown. Remove with a slotted spoon and place in a colander in the sink to drain.

SERVES 6

1 kg/2¼ lb boneless lamb, such as leg, well rinsed

2 tablespoons vegetable oil

2 onions, finely chopped   3–4 dried bay leaves

6 curry leaves, optional

2 cloves

2 green cardamom pods   2 cinnamon sticks

1 teaspoon cumin seeds

2 tablespoons Ginger and Garlic Paste (page 29)

4 teaspoons Kashmiri red chilli powder or cayenne pepper

2 teaspoons turmeric

1 tablespoon ground coriander   200 g/7 oz tomatoes, chopped

30 g/1 oz jaggery or dark brown sugar, dissolved in 2 tablespoons water

salt, to taste

1 teaspoon garam masala (page 28)

150 g/5 oz potato straws (see Introduction), to serve

chopped fresh coriander/cilantro leaves, to garnish

PLACE THE LAMB in a large saucepan with water to cover and bring to the boil. Meanwhile, heat the oil in a large pan or wok. Add the onions and stir-fry until they turn brown. Add the bay leaves, curry leaves, cloves, cardamom, cinnamon and cumin seeds and continue frying until the spices turn brown. Add the ginger and garlic paste, chilli powder, turmeric and ground coriander and continue cooking until the aroma of garlic is evident.

Add the lamb and its cooking liquid and bring to the boil. Lower the heat and simmer for 45–50 minutes until the lamb is cooked through and tender. Add water occasionally, if necessary. Stir in the tomatoes and bring the mixture to the boil, and continue boiling, stirring occasionally, until all the liquid evaporates and the gravy is thick. Stir in the jaggery, adjust the salt and sprinkle with the garam masala. Serve hot with potato straws on top and garnished with coriander/cilantro.

KID GOSHT
Parsi Baby Lamb Curry

TENDER BABY LAMB is cooked in a mild preparation, including cashew nuts and coconuts. This recipe includes dried red chillies, which give it heat, but substitute cherry tomatoes for a milder version. Freshly cooked basamati rice is the ideal accompaniment for this curry.

SERVES 4

1 kg/2¼ lb baby lamb, boned and cubed

6 green cardamom pods   4 dried bay leaves

2.5 cm/1 inch piece of cinnamon stick

1 teaspoon cloves

250 g/9 oz/2½ cups fresh coconut, grated

250 g/9 oz/1½ cups cashew nuts

2 tablespoons vegetable oil, plus extra for deep-frying the potatoes

60 g/2 oz/½ cup onions, chopped

2 teaspoons cumin seeds

2 tablespoons Ginger and Garlic Paste (page 29)

2 teaspoons chopped fresh green chillies

8–10 dried red chillies

200 g/7 oz potatoes, peeled and cut into 2.5 cm/1 inch cubes

1 tablespoon lime juice

1 teaspoon garam masala (page 28)

salt, to taste

PLACE THE LAMB in a large saucepan with the green cardamoms, bay leaves, cinnamon and cloves and bring to the boil. Meanwhile, place the coconut and cashew nuts in a blender or food processor and process until a fine paste forms. Heat the oil in a large saucepan. Add the onions and cumin seeds and stir-fry until the onions are light brown. Add the ginger and garlic paste and continue stir-frying until the aroma of cooked garlic is evident. Add the coconut and nut paste and stir in a little of the lamb cooking liquid to thin as necessary. Add the green chillies and red chillies. Use a slotted spoon to transfer the lamb, which should be quite tender by now, to the

pan. Add just enough cooking liquid to make a gravy and continue simmering.

Meanwhile, heat the oil for deep-frying the potatoes in a deep saucepan to 200°C/400°F, or until a cube of bread will brown in about 30 seconds. Add the potatoes, in batches if necessary, and deep-fry until golden brown. Remove with a slotted spoon and drain on crumpled kitchen paper/paper towels. Add the potatoes to the lamb curry and continue to simmer for about 10 minutes until they are tender. Sprinkle with the lime juice and garam masala. Add salt and serve.

GOSHT NU BAFFAT
Lamb and Vegetable Stew

THIS IS A VERY POPULAR SUNDAY BUFFET DISH at the Brasserie. It is lightly spiced, and ideal for young children, who are all over the restaurant at weekend lunches. Parsi cooks love to combine their lamb and chicken with vegetables.

SERVES 4

30 cashew nuts
750 g/1½ lb boneless lamb, diced
1 tablespooon Ginger and Garlic Paste (page 29)
2 tablespoons vegetable oil
6 green cardamom pods
1 teaspoon cumin seeds
1 large onion, finely sliced
225 ml/8 fl oz/1 cup thin coconut milk (page 32)
3 tablespoons natural yogurt (page 33), whisked
1 teaspoon turmeric

2 carrots, peeled and cut into 1 cm/½ inch cubes
2 large potaotes, peeled and cut into 1 cm/½ inch cubes
1 white radish/daikon, peeled and cut into 1 cm/½ inch cubes
150 g/5 oz/1 cup shelled peas
salt, to taste
225 ml/8 fl oz/1 cup thick coconut milk (page 32)
2–4 green chillies, chopped, to taste
2 teaspoons ground white pepper
2 teaspoons garam masala (page 28)
1 tablespoon chopped fresh coriander/cilantro, to garnish

SOAK THE CASHEW NUTS in water to just cover for about 30 minutes. Place the nuts and liquid in an electric blender and blend until a thick, smooth paste forms, then set aside. Meanwhile, place the lamb in a glass bowl with 1 tablespoon of the ginger and garlic paste and leave to marinate for 15–20 minutes.

Heat the oil in a large saucepan. Add the cardamoms and cumin seeds and stir-fry for about 30 seconds until they crackle. Stir in the onions and continue stir-frying until they are light brown. Add the lamb to the pan and continue stir-frying for 5–6 minutes until brown.

Stir in the nut paste, coconut milk, yogurt and turmeric. Fry over a medium heat for about 10 minutes, stirring occasionally, then add enough water to cover the lamb. Bring to the boil, stirring, then lower the heat and simmer for 20–25 minutes. Stir in the carrots, potato, white radish, peas and salt and continue cooking until the lamb and vegetables are tender, adding extra water to keep all the ingredients covered.

Add the thick coconut milk, chillies and ground white pepper. Adjust the salt if necessary. Stir together and simmer for a couple of minutes. Sprinkle with garam masala and serve garnished with the coriander/cilantro.

Ginger Root
and Mint on Cinnamon Bark

GOSHT DHANSAK
Spicy Lamb Curry with Lentil and Vegetable Purée

SEE PHOTOGRAPH ON PAGE 84

DHAN MEANS 'GRAIN OR RICE' and *sak* means 'vegetables', and *dhansak* is a traditional Parsi cooking style. It is also very popular for the Sunday family lunches here at the Brasserie. The lamb is always served with a special rice, and the two together are called *dhansak*. When we serve this as part of the Sunday buffet, fried lamb meat balls are served on the rice.

SERVES 4

900 g/2 lb leg of lamb, boned and cubed

6 green cardamom pods

6 bay leaves

1½ tablespoons Ginger and Garlic Paste (page 29)

salt, to taste

450 g/1 lb/3 cups yellow lentils, well rinsed

6 green chillies, chopped

6 sprigs fresh fenugreek leaves, chopped

4 sprigs fresh dill, chopped

3 sprigs fresh mint leaves, chopped

1 large aubergine/eggplant, peeled and cubed

7.5 cm/3 inch piece of pumpkin, peeled and cubed

1 teaspoon sugar

3 tablespoons vegetable oil

2 onions, sliced   6 garlic cloves, sliced

4 tablespoons shop-bought dhansak masala

1 tablespoon Kashmiri red chilli powder or cayenne pepper

½ tablespoon turmeric

½ tablespoon tamarind pulp (page 33)

salt, to taste

chopped fresh coriander/cilantro leaves, to garnish

1 quantity Dhansak Rice (page 81), to serve

PLACE THE LAMB, cardamoms, bay leaves, ginger and garlic paste and salt in a large saucepan. Add just enough water to cover and bring to the boil, then lower the heat and simmer for about 40 minutes until the lamb is tender. Skim the surface as necessary. In another saucepan, place the lentils with 2½ times their volume in water. Bring to the boil and add the chillies, half the fenugreek leaves, the dill, mint, aubergine/eggplant, pumpkin and sugar. Continue boiling until the vegetables and lentils are very tender, adding a little extra water if necessary. Transfer to an electric blender or food processor and process to a smooth paste that is not too runny.

Heat the oil in another large pan. Add the onions and fry until they are light brown. Remove about three-quarters of the onions and drain on crumpled kitchen paper/paper towels; reserve for the garnish. Add the garlic to the onions remaining in the pan and stir-fry until the aroma of cooked garlic is evident. Stir in the remaining frenugreek leaves, dhansak masala, chilli powder and turmeric and stir-fry for a further 2 minutes. Add the tamarind pulp and continue cooking for about 3 minutes, stirring. Stir in the lentil and vegetable paste. Bring to the boil, adding a few ladlefuls of lamb stock. Use a slotted spoon to transfer the lamb from its cooking liquid to this mixture. If necessary, add a bit more cooking liquid, but this should be a thick curry. Add salt cautiously because the cooking liquid has salt in it.

Serve garnished with coriander/cilantro and some of the reserved browned onions. Accompany with the rice and meatballs and put the remaining brown onions over them.

DHANSAK RICE
Parsi-Spiced Rice with Lamb Meatballs

SEE PHOTOGRAPH ON PAGE 84

ALSO OCCASIONALLY CALLED BROWN RICE, this is the traditional accompaniment to Parsi lamb curry with lentil purée. The brown comes from the sugar with the onions, and the dhansak masala gives it the typical flavour. This rice can also be served with *dal*.

SERVES 4

750 g/1½ lb/3¾ cups basmati rice
2 tablespoons vegetable oil
1 large onion, sliced   1 tablespoon sugar
6 cloves   6 star anise
4 bay leaves
5 cm/2 inch piece of cinnamon stick
1 tablespoon shop-bought dhansak masala
2 teaspoons cumin seeds
salt, to taste

FOR THE LAMB MEATBALLS
225 g/8 oz minced/ground lamb
2 green chillies, finely chopped
2 sprigs fresh coriander/cilantro leaves, finely chopped
1 egg
1 cm/½ inch piece of fresh root ginger, peeled and finely chopped
1 teaspoon turmeric
salt, to taste
vegetable oil for deep-frying

WASH THE RICE by putting it in a large bowl and covering with water, then stir and drain off the water. Repeat 3 or 4 times until the water remains clear. Cover with fresh water and leave to soak for 30 minutes. Heat the oil in a large flameproof casserole with a tight-fitting lid. Add the onion and fry until light brown, then stir in the sugar and continue frying until the sugar caramelizes and the onion turns very dark brown.

Quickly stir in the cloves, star anise, bay leaves, cinnamon, dhansak masala and cumin seeds. Add the drained rice and stir-fry for 1 minute. Add salt and enough water to come 2.5 cm/ 1 inch above the surface of the rice. Bring to the boil and cook until the rice swells up to the water level. Cover the casserole and cook in an oven preheated to 220°C/425°F/Gas

7 for about 20 minutes until the rice is completely cooked and tender.

Meanwhile, to make the meatballs, chop all the ingredients together or mince/grind in a meat mincer/grinder or process in a food processor. Add salt to taste. Shape into 12 marble-size meat balls and poach in boiling water for 1–2 minutes until cooked through. Remove from the water and drain well. Heat the oil in a saucepan to 180°C/350°F, or until a cube of bread will brown in about 45 seconds. Add the meatballs, in batches, and deep-fry until golden brown. Drain well on crumpled kitchen paper/paper towels. When the rice is ready, use a spatula to loosen some of the grains. Serve it garnished with the lamb kababs.

SAAS NI MACCHI
Fish in Sauce, Parsi Style

SEE PHOTOGRAPH ON PAGE 85

IN INDIA, I would use pomfret for this delicate dish, but cod and halibut are good substitutes. Pomfret, however, is sold frozen in almost all Thai and Chinese supermarkets. If you use pomfret, leave it to thaw, then cut the fish into steaks, discarding the head and fins. Alternatively, use skinless fillets of other fish.

SERVES 4

900 g/2 lb pomfret, cut into 2.5 cm/1 inch darnes or steaks, or cod or halibut

fillets, skinned and cut into 5 cm/2 inch cubes

1 tablespoon lemon juice

salt, to taste

200 g/7 oz rice flour

4 egg whites

4 tablespoons distilled white vinegar

2 tablespoons sugar

2 teaspoons chopped fresh mint

10–12 curry leaves, optional

2 tablespoons vegetable oil

4 teaspoons Ginger and Garlic Paste (page 29)

2 teaspoons chopped fresh green chillies

1 teaspoon cumin seeds

1 teaspoon garam masala (page 28)

salt, to taste

3 tomatoes, sliced, to garnish

PUT THE FISH IN A GLASS BOWL. Add the lemon juice and salt and leave to marinate for 10–15 minutes. Meanwhile, whisk together the rice flour, egg whites, vinegar and sugar. Stir in the mint and 6 of the curry leaves and whisk well; set aside. Heat the oil in a large saucepan. Add the remaining curry leaves, ginger and garlic paste and chillies and stir-fry until the aroma of cooked garlic is evident. Stir in 1.2 litres/2 pints/5 cups water and bring to the boil. Lower the heat, add the fish and simmer until it is cooked through and the flesh flakes easily when tested with the tip of a knife. Remove from the liquid and keep warm.

Stir the rice flour mixture into the cooking liquid and simmer for 8–10 minutes, whisking frequently with a wire whisk. Do not let it boil or the egg white will curdle. Return the fish to the sauce and stir in the cumin, garam masala and salt. The sauce should be sweet, sour and spicy. Serve garnished with sliced tomatoes.

MARGI NI CURRY
Spicy Chicken Curry, Parsi Style

SEE PHOTOGRAPH ON PAGE 84

THE PARSI ACCENT in this simple curry is the use of the combination of peanuts, coconuts and red chillies. Each Parsi family will cook this dish slightly differently, and this is my favourite version from the Dubash family in Bombay.

SERVES 4

6 dried red chillies, or 1 tablespoon Kashmiri red chilli powder or cayenne pepper

1 tablespoon shelled and peeled peanuts

2 teaspoons yellow gram or channa dal

1 teaspoon coriander seeds   ½ teaspoon cumin seeds

2 tablespoons vegetable oil

2 onions, sliced

1 tablespoon Ginger and Garlic Paste (page 29)

1 chicken, about 1.5 kg/3½ lb, skinned, boned and cut into 4 cm/1½ inch pieces

2 tomatoes, chopped

225 ml/8 fl oz/1 cup thick coconut milk (page 32)

1 tablespoon tamarind pulp (page 33)

2 teaspoons jaggery or dark brown sugar, dissolved in 2 tablespoons water

salt, to taste

boiled basmati rice, to serve

PLACE THE CHILLIES, peanuts, yellow gram, coriander seeds and cumin seeds in a dry skillet/frying pan and heat over a very low heat, stirring constantly, until the aroma of the spices wafts up. Transfer the spices to an electric spice mill and grind until a fine powder forms; set aside.

Heat the oil in a large saucepan. Add the onion and fry until golden brown. Stir in the ginger and garlic paste and continue frying until the aroma of cooked garlic is evident. Add the ground spices and fry for a further 1–2 minutes, stirring briskly. Add the chicken pieces to the pan and stir-fry for 3–4 minutes to brown. Stir in the tomatoes and 225 ml/8 fl oz/1 cup water, cover and simmer for 20–25 minutes until the chicken is cooked through and tender. Stir in the coconut milk, tamarind, jaggery and salt and bring to a rolling boil. Adjust the seasoning and serve.

BADAMI MARGI
Chicken Curry with Almonds

A FAVOURITE DISH for all youngsters and anyone who comes to the Brasserie but is actually 'chilli shy'. Yet, if you want to spice it up to be firey hot, add some chopped green chillies.

SERVES 4

100 g/4 oz/1 cup blanched almonds and cashew nuts mixed
1 tablespoon vegetable oil
6 black peppercorns
5 green cardamom pods
2.5 cm/1 inch piece of cinnamon stick
1 large onion, chopped
2 teaspoons Ginger and Garlic Paste (page 29)
2 potatoes, peeled and quartered
1 chicken, about 1.5 kg/3½ lb, skinned, boned and cut into
4 cm/1½ inch pieces
450 ml/16 fl oz/2 cups thick coconut milk (page 32)
salt, to taste
chopped fresh coriander/cilantro leaves, to garnish

SOAK THE ALMONDS and cashew nuts in water to just cover for 30 minutes. Place the nuts and liquid in an electric blender and blend until a thick, smooth paste forms; set aside. Heat the oil in a large saucepan. Add the peppercorns, cardamoms and cinnamon and stir-fry for less than a minute until the cardamoms start to brown. Add the onion and fry until golden brown. Stir in the ginger and garlic paste and continue stir-frying for about 1 minute until the aroma of cooked garlic is evident, then stir in the nut paste; stir constantly as the mixture tends to stick. Stir 100 ml/4 fl oz/½ cup water and simmer for about 3 minutes, then add the potatoes and continue simmering, stirring, for 2 minutes.

Add the chicken and continue simmering and stirring for about 5 minutes until until the chicken and potatoes are half cooked. Add the coconut milk, salt and another 100 ml/4 fl oz/ ½ cup water and continue simmering for about 20 minutes until the chicken is cooked through and tender. The gravy should be semi-thick and not too thin. Serve garnished with coriander/cilantro.

PREVIOUS SPREAD, clockwise from bottom left: Gosht Dhansak (*page 80*); Dhansak Rice (*page 81*); Margi Ni Curry (*page 83*); Saas Ni Macchi (*page 82*); Sali Boti (*page 76*).

GOSHT NU PULAO
Parsi Lamb Pulao
SEE PHOTOGRAPH ON PAGE 136

THIS COMBINATION of marinated lamb with basmati rice is a
Parsi speciality. Once when this was being cooked, an early guest
smelt the aroma wafting through to the bar area a good 50 metres
away through two sets of doors. Of course he ordered it for his
dinner, and now always asks for it.

SERVES 4

450 g/1 lb boneless lamb, cut into 2.5 cm/1 inch cubes
225 ml/8 fl oz/1 cup natural yogurt (page 44)
1 tablespoon Ginger and Garlic Paste (page 29)
2 teaspoons Kashmiri red chilli powder or cayenne pepper
2 teaspoons garam masala (page 28)
1 teaspoon ground cumin
½ teaspoon turmeric
450 g/1 lb/2¼ cups basmati rice
25 g/1 oz/2 tablespoons ghee

1 large onion, sliced
3 large potatoes, peeled and quartered
salt, to taste
6 black peppercorns
4 cloves   3 bay leaves
2.5 cm/1 inch piece of cinnamon stick
1 tablespoon vegetable oil
1 teaspoon saffron dissolved in 1 tablespoon milk
chopped fresh coriander/cilantro leaves, to garnish

PLACE THE LAMB in a glass bowl. Add the yogurt, ginger and
garlic paste, chilli powder, garam masala, ground cumin and
turmeric and leave to marinate at room temperature for
3 hours or overnight in the refrigerator. Meanwhile, wash the
rice by putting it in a large bowl and covering with water, then
drain off the cloudy water. Repeat 3 or 4 times until the water
remains clear. Cover with fresh water and leave to soak for
30 minutes.

Melt the ghee in a deep flameproof casserole with a tight-
fitting lid. Add the onion and fry until light brown. Transfer
half to crumpled kitchen paper/paper towels to drain; reserve
for the garnish. Add the lamb with its marinade to the casserole and stir-fry for 6–8 minutes. Stir in the potatoes and
continue stir-frying for a further 3–4 minutes. Add just
enough warm water to cover the meat and simmer, uncovered,

for about 45 minutes until the lamb is cooked through and
tender and the gravy just coats it, but isn't runny. Stir in salt;
set aside.

Bring a large saucepan of water, about 3 times the volume of
the rice, to the boil. Add the peppercorns, cloves, bay leaves,
cinnamon, vegetable oil and salt. When the water is boiling,
stir in the drained rice and return to the boil until the rice is
half cooked. Test the rice by pressing a grain between your
fingers: the centre should be white and powdery. Drain
through a large sieve/strainer. Spoon the rice on top of the
lamb in the casserole. Pour in the milk and saffron. Cover the
casserole and cook in an oven preheated to 190°C/375°F/Gas
5 for 35–40 minutes. To serve, spoon out the rice and place
some lamb on top. Sprinkle the reserved brown onions on top
and serve garnished with the coriander/cilantro.

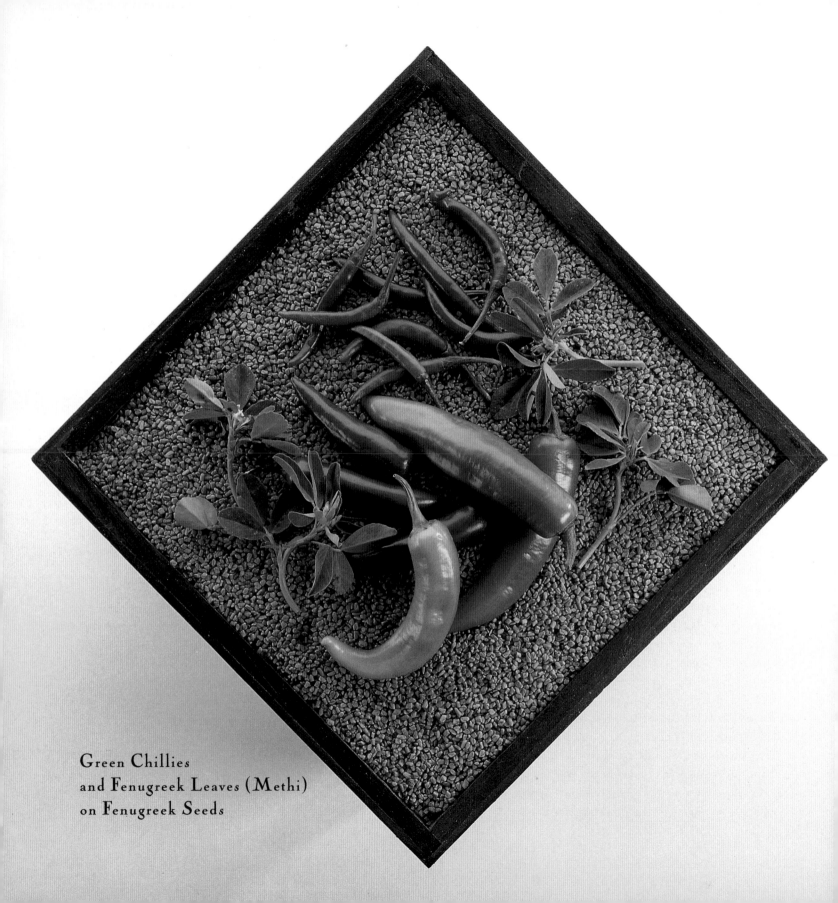

Green Chillies
and Fenugreek Leaves (Methi)
on Fenugreek Seeds

Goan Specialities

GOA, THE STATE TO THE SOUTH OF MAHARASHTRA on the western coast of India, is a lush green land with a beautiful coastline that is increasingly popular with tourists from all over the world. India's smallest state, it was long colonized by the Portuguese and a large percentage of the population are Christians. The Goans are hard-working people, traditionally fishermen and farmers. They tap their palm or coconut juice fresh from their trees for an early morning drink called a *neera*. The same juice ferments in the heat of the sun to become *toddy*, a potent brew. Palm and cashew are also distilled to make the famous *feni*, of which there are many proprietary brands. Goa produces wine and port as well.

Goan cooking is a heady art. The ingredients are very fresh and chefs have a lot of creative leeway with the recipes. The cuisine, like the culture of the state, blends elements of Portuguese and Indian, and the Goans are justifiably proud of it. Coconut is used extensively and forms the basis of many Goan masalas. The seafood is superb and locally caught by the descendants of the original Konkani fisher-folk. The meat is typically pork, served many different ways including roasted; the offal is used too, producing the Goan sausages that are unique in Indian cuisine and so typical of the region. The pork sausages are smoked with spices, then re-cooked. The Alphonso mango which grows in Goa is prized throughout India and across the world. As part of my chef's training I worked at the Taj Holiday Village and Fort Aguada hotels alongside some wonderful Goan chefs who could speak only Portuguese and the local dialect of Konkani.

Stone grinding is very important in producing Goan masalas. Fresh, grated coconut, used extensively in Goan recipes, has its own natural oils, and because an electric blender tends to heat up the mixture, unless you're careful you will find the oil separating. The moment you start cooking the masala, you get the oil on top, and the coconut at the bottom. Stone grinding is a longer but colder method of grinding, producing a curry that is absolutely stable with no oil on top. If you're using fresh coconut in a domestic blender, always blend the masala dry first, then add the liquid slowly to make a mash, then a fine paste.

Goan food can be hot: the Goan chilli is very potent, particularly the seeds. At the Brasserie we import them, but at home you will have to use chilli powder or dried chillis.

Another distinctive Goan ingredient is *cocum*, a fruit like a round berry. The Goans salt it, dry it in the sun, and deseed it. The result – like an almost black pea – is used as a souring agent, most typically in the Goan prawn curry, the staple of the region. Any good Indian grocer should be able to get *cocum* for you.

NISTEACHI KODI
Goan Fish Curry
SEE PHOTOGRAPH ON PAGE 93

THIS IS THE MOST POPULAR DISH of the region, eaten almost every day by native Goans. It's always served with steaming boiled rice, and made from the catch of the day. I make it with pomfret, a delicate flat fish with few tiny scales, but mackerel or almost any fresh fish will do. I have also used skinned fillets of halibut, which turns out well.

SERVES 6

4 pomfret, scaled with fins cut away and filleted

2 tablespoons lemon juice

salt, to taste

20 dried red chillies   4 garlic cloves

3 fresh coconuts, grated

2 tablespoons coriander seeds

1½ tablespoons turmeric   1 tablespoon cumin seeds

2.5 cm/1 inch piece of fresh root ginger, peeled

2 tablespoons vegetable oil

2 onions, sliced

1½ tablespoons tamarind pulp (page 33)

4 green chillies, split

PLACE THE POMFRET in a glass dish. Add the lemon juice and salt; set aside. Place the red chillies, garlic, coconut, coriander seeds, turmeric, cumin seeds and ginger in a blender or food processor; add a little hot water. Process to a smooth paste.

Heat the oil in a large frying pan/skillet. Add the onions and stir-fry until light brown. Add the tamarind pulp and simmer for about 10 minutes, stirring occasionally. Add the green chillies and masala paste and continue simmering over a low heat for about 20 minutes. Add the pomfret fillets and simmer until the fish is cooked through and the flesh flakes easily when tested with the tip of a knife. Add a little boiling water if necessary to thin the sauce. Adjust the seasoning if necessary and serve with rice.

SHRIMP BALCHAO
Stir-Fried Shrimp in Spicy Goan Masala

YOU CAN USE small shrimp or larger prawns for *balchao*. At the Bombay Brasserie, I use the smaller shrimp because they absorb the flavours so well. The basic red masala is fiery, almost like a pickle. It is ground without water so the shelf life is long if you keep it in an airtight container at room temperature; you will only need about half for this recipe. This *balchao* is normally served as an accompaniment to other Goan dishes.

SERVES 4

3 tablespoons vegetable oil

1 kg/2¼ lb small raw shrimp, shelled and deveined

500 g/18 oz/3½ cups onions, chopped

10–12 garlic cloves, chopped

12 curry leaves, optional

2 tomatoes, chopped

1 raw mango, peeled and chopped, optional

2 teaspoons turmeric

salt, to taste

FOR THE RED MASALA

75 g/3 oz whole dry red chillies or 2–3 tablespoons Kashmiri red chilli powder
or cayenne pepper

7.5 cm/3 inch piece of cinnamon stick

2.5 cm/1 inch piece of fresh root ginger, peeled

20 cloves   8 green cardamom pods

7 garlic cloves   1½ pieces of mace

1 teaspoon black peppercorns

vinegar for grinding, preferably Goan coconut vinegar, or malt or distilled
white vinegar

TO MAKE THE MASALA, put all the ingredients in a blender or food processor and process until a thick paste forms, adding the vinegar as necessary to help all the ingredients blend well together. Heat the vegetable oil in a large frying pan/skillet until very hot. Add the shrimp, working in batches if necessary, and stir-fry until they turn pink. Remove the shrimp from the pan.

Using the same oil, add the onions, garlic and curry leaves and fry, stirring occasionally, for 3–4 minutes. Add the tomatoes and continue frying for 2 minutes. Stir in 4 tablespoons of the masala and simmer over a low heat for 10 minutes. Return the shrimp to the pan with the chopped mango, turmeric and salt. Stir well then simmer long enough to warm the shrimp through before serving.

PRAWN MASALA
King Prawn/Jumbo Shrimp Masala
SEE PHOTOGRAPH ON PAGE 92

ALWAYS A FAVOURITE at the Taj Holiday Village in Goa, and here at the Brasserie. Even if we take it off the menu occasionally, special orders keep coming in.

SERVES 4

20 large raw prawns/shrimp, shelled and deveined

juice of 2 lemons

salt, to taste

2 tablespoons vegetable oil

1 large onion, chopped

1 tablespoon Ginger and Garlic Paste (page 29)

6 whole green chillies

3 tablespoons Red Masala (page 91)

1 tablespoon tomato purée/paste

2 teaspoons turmeric

chopped fresh coriander/cilantro, to garnish

PLACE THE PRAWNS/SHRIMP in a glass bowl and sprinkle with half the lemon juice and the salt, then set aside for 10–15 minutes. Heat the oil in a *kadai* or wok. Add the onions and fry until they just start to turn golden brown. Add the ginger and garlic paste and continue frying until the aroma of garlic is evident. Stir in the chillies, red masala, tomato purée/paste and turmeric and stir-fry for 3–4 minutes. Add the prawns and stir into the masala mixture and simmer for 12–15 minutes until the prawns turn pink and curl. Sprinkle with a little water, if necessary, to prevent them sticking. Add salt and sprinkle with the remaining lemon juice. Serve garnished with coriander/ cilantro.

PREVIOUS SPREAD, clockwise from top left: basmati rice; Galinha Cafreal (*page 98*); Lobster Peri Peri (*page 95*); Nisteachi Kodi (*page 90*); Prawn Masala (*page 94*).

LOBSTER PERI PERI
Pan-fried Lobster with Red Masala

SEE PHOTOGRAPH ON PAGE 93

THE BEST OPTION is to buy your lobster live and have your fish-monger cut and prepare it for you. Otherwise, use a heavy and sharp knife to trim off the small feet and feelers next to the claws, then split the tail in half from head to tail. The best way to do this is in two stages – vertically pierce the tip of your knife into the segment between the head and the tail. Turn the knife down-wards and press with your hand to cut through the shell; reverse the blade and repeat on the other half. Use the back of the knife to crush the shell on the claws. All this is very neatly done at the Brasserie using an electric bandsaw, but at home it can be more difficult, which is why I suggest you have the fishmonger do it. This recipe is equally delicious cooked on a barbecue.

SERVES 4

4 live lobsters, each about 450 g/1 lb, prepared (see Introduction)

juice of 1 lemon

salt, to taste

6 tablespoons Red Masala (page 91)

2 tablespoons vegetable oil

lemon wedges, to serve

REMOVE THE VISCERA and intestinal veins from the lobster tails if necessary, then rinse well and pat dry with kitchen paper/paper towels. Place the lobsters in a glass dish and sprinkle with the lemon juice and salt and set aside for 10 minutes. Liberally apply the red masala to the exposed tail flesh and the crushed claws and set aside again for a further 10 minutes.

Heat the oil in a large saucepan. Add the lobster, in batches if necessary, flesh side down. (A word of warning – turn down the heat and shut any overhead extractor fan before adding the lobsters because flames tend to shoot up.) Fry the lobsters on one side for 2 minutes, then flip them over and fry them shell side down for 6–8 minutes until the flesh is tender and the shells turn red. Serve hot, with lemon wedges.

GOSHT XACUTI
Lamb with Coconut and Spices, Goan Style

A *XACUTI* is one of the most complicated of the Goan dishes, made differently by the Christians and Hindus. The Hindu version is the darkest and smoothest. It can also be made with chicken pieces. This is painstaking to make, but well worth the effort. Collect all the spices first and prepare the dish in stages.

SERVES 4

3 tablespoons vegetable oil

2 onions, thinly sliced

2 coconuts, grated

10 black peppercorns

6–8 dried red chillies

6 cloves

6 garlic cloves

4 green cardamom pods

2 star anise

1½ pieces of mace

½ nutmeg, grated

1 tablespoon coriander seeds

4 teaspoons poppy seeds

2 teaspoons cumin seeds

½ teaspoon fennel seeds

2.5 cm/1 inch piece of fresh root ginger, peeled and chopped

¾ teaspoon turmeric

1 tablespoon raw rice grains

1 tablespoon tamarind pulp (page 33)

6 green chillies, slit

900 g/2 lb boneless lamb, cubed

salt, to taste

HEAT 1 TABLESPOON OF THE OIL in a large frying pan/skillet. Add half the onions and fry, stirring frequently, until light brown. Add the coconut, peppercorns, chillies, cloves, garlic, cardamom, star anise, mace, nutmeg, coriander seeds, poppy seeds, cumin seeds, fennel seeds, ginger, turmeric and rice. Continue frying over a low heat, stirring often, until the whole mixture is light brown and aromatic. Take care while roasting the coconut because it should be brown, but it can easily burn. Transfer the mixture to a blender or food processor and process until a thick paste forms, adding about 225 ml/8 fl oz/ 1 cup hot water if necessary. Add the tamarind pulp.

Heat the remaining 2 tablespoons of oil in a large saucepan. Add the remaining onions and the green chillies and stir-fry until the onions are light brown. Add the lamb and stir-fry until they are brown all over and the natural liquid it gives up starts to dry up. Stir in the paste and continue cooking for about 10 minutes, stirring frequently.

Add salt and enough hot water to cover the lamb and bring to the boil, then boil gently until the lamb is cooked through and tender; the gravy should be medium thick. Check the salt again before serving.

Baby Corn
on Black Pepper Corns

GALINHA CAFREAL
Pan-Fried Chicken with Green Herbs

SEE PHOTOGRAPH ON PAGE 92

THIS PAN-FRIED CHICKEN DISH is traditionally served in Goa with rounds of fried potatoes and a mound of garlic-flavoued rice. The skin of the chicken should be crisp. At the Bombay Brasserie I have also made this with poussins, and they soak up the marinade very well.

SERVES 4

1 chicken, about 1.5 kg/3½ lb, quartered with the skin left on

juice of ½ lime

salt, to taste

2 tablespoons vegetable oil

2 potatoes, peeled and sliced 1 cm/½ inch thick

FOR THE GREEN MASALA

6 green chillies

6 garlic cloves

2 green cardamom pods

2 cloves

1 bunch fresh coriander/cilantro leaves, chopped

2.5 cm/1 inch piece of fresh root ginger, peeled

2 tablespoons Goan, malt or distilled white vinegar

1 teaspoon sugar

½ teaspoon cumin seeds

½ teaspoon turmeric

juice of ½ lime

PIERCE THE CHICKEN PIECES all over with a fork. Place them in a glass dish with the lime juice and salt; set aside. Place all the ingredients for the masala in a blender or food processor and process until a fine paste forms. Spread this masala all over the chicken pieces and set aside to marinate for at least 2 hours at room temperature.

Heat the oil in a large frying pan/skillet. Add the chicken pieces and fry for 10–12 minutes until the skin is dark brown and crispy and the juices run clear when each piece is pricked with the tip of a knife. Turn over the pieces several times while they are frying. Halfway through the cooking process, arrange the potatoes in a ring around the chicken so they fry with the chicken. Or, they can be fried in the fat remaining in the pan after the chicken is removed. Serve hot with the potatoes arranged around the chicken.

SUNGTACHI CUTLETS
Prawn Cutlets

THESE CUTLETS are a delightful accompaniment to Goan Fish Curry and rice. They are very much like crisp hash browns, and can also be served as a pre-dinner snack.

MAKES 8

450 g/1 lb shelled prawns, deveined and washed
1 small onion, peeled and chopped
2 green chillies, chopped
6 sprigs coriander leaves, chopped
3 garlic cloves, peeled and chopped
1 cm/½ inch ginger, chopped
salt to taste
½ teaspoon ground black pepper
1 teaspoon Garam Masala (page 28)
½ teaspoon turmeric powder
juice of ½ lemon
2 eggs
2 slices of white bread soaked in water
breadcrumbs to coat
vegetable oil for frying

PUT THE PRAWNS, onion, chillies, coriander, garlic and ginger into a food processor and chop until very fine. Add the salt, pepper, Garam Masala, turmeric, lemon juice, and soaked bread. Mix thoroughly and shape into 8 round flat patties. Break the eggs into a bowl and whisk. Dip the patties one by one into the egg and then coat with breadcrumbs. Heat oil in a frying pan to 180°C/350°F or until a cube of bread browns in about 45 seconds in it. Fry the patties till they are golden brown and cooked through. Serve immediately, as re-heating will make them soggy.

PORK VINDALOO
Pork Vindaloo

THE MUCH-MALIGNED VINDALOO is a very traditional Goan pork dish made with a traditional red masala with vinegar. This is a fiery dish, but as it should be made several hours before eating the vinegar mellows the heat.

SERVES 4

900 g/2 lb boneless pork, cubed with a thin layer of fat left on
3 tablespoons Red Masala (page 91)
1 tablespoon vegetable oil
2 onions, sliced
2 tomatoes, finely chopped
2 tablespoons Goan, malt or distilled white vinegar
2 large potatoes, peeled and cut into large fingers
15–18 pickled cocktail onions, drained
salt, to taste

PLACE THE PORK in a glass bowl. Add the red masala, stir well and set aside to marinate for about 1 hour at room temperature or 4 hours in the refrigerator. Heat the oil in a large saucepan. Add the onions and fry until they are soft and translucent. Stir in the tomatoes and cook for 2 minutes, stirring frequently. Add the pork and cook, stirring frequently, for 10 minutes without adding any additional liquid.

Stir in the vinegar and enough water to cover the pork and bring to the boil. Lower the heat and simmer for 12–15 minutes. Add the potatoes and cocktail onions and continue simmering until the potatoes are tender and the pork is cooked through and tender. Add salt. Allow this to stand for at least several hours before re-heating and serving.

Okra (Ladies' Fingers)
on Mace

Moghlai Specialities

THE RULE OF THE MOGHULS in northern India began in 1526, with the taking of the throne at Delhi by Babur, King of Kabul. The Muslim dynasty that followed dominated northern India for 300 years. The Moghuls were great administrators and builders – Shah Jahan's Taj Mahal is the finest testimony to their skills. But they were also great cooks and, despite their religion, lovers of wine as well as food.

The royal kitchens of the Moghul emperors were elaborate and heavily staffed affairs, capable of preparing over 100 dishes at short notice for the Emperor, his harem and honoured guests. In a Moghul banquet the cooks would use exotic imported spices, and new ingredients like nuts, which were not used in Indian cooking before and which gave body to gravies. On a recent visit to northern India I was very knowledgeably guided through a tour of the palaces and fortresses of the Moghuls. Even after remaining disused for a few centuries, their kitchens still impart a sensation of the frantic preparation for banquets,

scurrying kitchen hands and the great chefs – the *ustaads* – painstakingly stirring the massive cauldrons of *kormas* and *yakhnis*.

The cuisine spread from the original Moghul strongholds of Delhi and the far north, and today a lot of food in North India retains a strong Moghlai accent. One important and distinctive style of Moghul cooking comes from Hydrabad in Central India, from the Nizaams, the local Muslim rulers who were connoisseurs of good food. Each would have his own kitchens and cooks and jealously guarded his culinary reputation.

In modern Bombay the Moghlai accent crept in with the advent of eating out at restaurants. Moghlai cooking was introduced through Punjabi restaurateurs, who opened eating houses and then very profitably conducted business serving Moghlai food. A few of them – like Delhi Darbar and Khyber – still flourish. It's also very much the cuisine that came into Britain when the Indian restaurant trade started here.

ROGAN JOSH
Lamb Curry, Kashmiri Style

SEE PHOTOGRAPH ON PAGE 104

ALTHOUGH TRADITIONALLY KASHMIRI, this was absorbed and spread by the Moghuls. It's supposed to be coloured a dark, rich red by a spice and a dye called *rattanjog* , made from the bark of a tree native to Kashmir, it is very much like a thin version of cinnamon bark. It is also very expensive: the substitute we use at the Brasserie is saffron, which gives a rich flavour.

SERVES 4

6 tomatoes, chopped

2 onions, chopped

2 tablespoons vegetable oil

1 tablespoon Ginger and Garlic Paste (page 29)

2 tablespoons ground coriander

1½ tablespoons Kashmiri red chilli powder or cayenne pepper

2 teaspoons turmeric

450 ml/16 fl oz/2 cups natural yogurt (page 33)

900 g/2 lb boneless leg of lamb, trimmed and cut into cubes

1 tablespoon garam masala (page 28)

1 tablespoon tomato purée/paste

2 teaspoons ground ginger

1 teaspoon Mace, Nutmeg and Green Cardamom Powder (page 29)

½ teaspoon saffron dissolved in 1 tablespoon warm milk

salt, to taste

chopped fresh coriander/cilantro leaves, to garnish

PLACE THE TOMATOES AND ONIONS in a blender or food processor and blend together until a paste forms; set aside. Heat the oil in a flameproof casserole or saucepan. Add the ginger and garlic paste and fry until the aroma of cooked garlic is evident. Add the tomato and onion paste, ground coriander, chilli powder and turmeric and fry over a low heat, stirring constantly; after 12–15 minutes the fat will separate.

Gradually stir in the yogurt, then add the lamb. Simmer, stirring occasionally, for 30 minutes. Add a little water if necessary, but the lamb should give off so much natural juice that extra liquid probably won't be needed. Stir in the garam masala and tomato purée/paste and continue simmering for 10–12 minutes until the lamb is cooked through and tender. Stir in the ground ginger, the mace, nutmeg and green cardamom powder, dissolved saffron and salt. Skim off any excess oil floating on the surface. Serve garnished with the coriander/cilantro.

GOSHT PASANDA
Stuffed Lamb Escalopes in Mild Cashew Sauce

SEE PHOTOGRAPH ON PAGE 105

IN INDIAN COOKING, a *pasanda* is a particular cut of meat, cut against the grain, from the thigh or calf. It is like an escalope, but not beaten before it is cooked. This can be stuffed and wrapped or stewed, and it is traditionally served with a mild *korma* sauce. Buy the leg escalopes from your butcher, or bone a leg of lamb and slice the large thigh muscle against the grain.

SERVES 4

30 cashew nuts

12 lamb escalopes from the thigh, about 700 g/1½ lb total weight

2 teaspoons ground white pepper   salt, to taste

100 g/4 oz paneer, grated

3 green chillies, finely chopped

2 sprigs fresh coriander/cilantro leaves, finely chopped

1 sprig fresh mint, finely chopped

0.5 cm/¼ inch piece of fresh root ginger, peeled and finely chopped

1 tablespoon shelled pistachio nuts, finely chopped

10 g/⅓ oz/2 teaspoons butter

1 tablespoon vegetable oil

1 large onion, finely chopped

½ tablespoon Ginger and Garlic Paste (page 29)

225 ml/8 fl oz/1 cup natural yogurt (page 33)

2 green chillies, finely chopped

2 tablespoons single/light cream

2 teaspoons Mace, Nutmeg and Cardamom Powder (page 29)

1 teaspoon ground white pepper

½ teaspoon saffron

chopped fresh coriander leaves, to garnish

SOAK THE CASHEW NUTS in water to just cover for 30 minutes. Place the nuts and liquid in an electric spice mill and grind until a thick, smooth paste forms; set aside.

Meanwhile, place the lamb escalopes on the work surface/countertop. Sprinkle with the pepper and salt. Place the paneer, chillies, coriander, mint, ginger and pistachio nuts in a bowl and knead firmly together. Shape the mixture into 12 equal baton shapes, then place a portion on top of each piece of lamb. Fold over the lamb and secure with a wooden cocktail stick/toothpick. Arrange the lamb rolls in a single layer in a large baking tray. Pour over 450 ml/16 fl oz/2 cups water and add the butter. Cover the backing tray and its contents with foil and cook in an oven preheated to 200°C/400°F/Gas 6 for 20 minutes, shaking the tray occasionally.

While the lamb is cooking, heat the oil in a large saucepan. Add the onion and fry until it is golden brown. Add the ginger and garlic paste and continue frying until the aroma of cooked garlic is evident. Gradually stir in the yogurt, then add the cashew paste, green chillies and 225 ml/8 fl oz/1 cup water. Bring to the boil, stirring constantly, then lower the heat and simmer for 10–12 minutes, stirring.

Transfer the lamb rolls to the sauce and add 225 ml/8 fl oz/1 cup of the cooking liquid to the sauce. Stir in the cream, the mace, nutmeg and green cardamom powder, white pepper and saffron. Swirl around the pan and add salt. Cover and simmer for 4–5 minutes until the lamb is cooked through and tender; check by removing and cutting through one roll. Serve garnished with chopped coriander/cilantro. Remove the wooden cocktail stick/toothpick before serving.

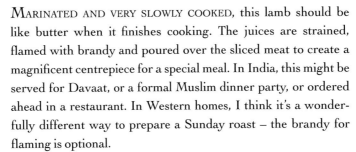

RAAN
Roast Leg of Lamb with Tandoori Masala
SEE PHOTOGRAPH ON PAGE 104

MARINATED AND VERY SLOWLY COOKED, this lamb should be like butter when it finishes cooking. The juices are strained, flamed with brandy and poured over the sliced meat to create a magnificent centrepiece for a special meal. In India, this might be served for Davaat, or a formal Muslim dinner party, or ordered ahead in a restaurant. In Western homes, I think it's a wonderfully different way to prepare a Sunday roast – the brandy for flaming is optional.

SERVES 4–6

1 leg of lamb, knuckle and hip bone removed
2 tablespoons Ginger and Garlic Paste (page 29)
3 tablespoons mustard or vegetable oil
20 shelled cashew nuts
900 ml/1½ pints/4 cups natural yogurt (page 33)
1 tablespoon Kashmiri red chilli powder or cayenne pepper

1 tablespoon tomato purée/paste
2 teaspoons garam masala (page 28)
1 teaspoon turmeric
2 tablespoons brandy
1 tablespoon single/light cream
sliced onions and lemon wedges, to garnish

USE THE TIP OF A KNIFE to make gashes all over the lamb. Rub in 1 tablespoon of the ginger and garlic paste and 1 tablespoon of the mustard oil. Place in a large ovenproof dish and leave to marinate for 30 minutes. Meanwhile, soak the cashew nuts in water to just cover for 30 minutes. Place the nuts and liquid in an electric blender and blend until a thick, smooth paste forms; set aside. Mix the cashew paste with the yogurt, remaining ginger and garlic paste, remaining mustard oil, the chilli powder, tomato purée/paste, garam masala and turmeric in a large bowl and whisk together well. Pour the mixture over the lamb and rub in. Cover and leave to marinate at room temperature for 4 hours or overnight in the refrigerator.

If the leg has been refrigerated, let it come up to room temperature before roasting. Cover with foil and roast in an oven preheated to 220°C/425°F/Gas 7 for 2–2½ hours, turning the leg and basting every 20 minutes, until the meat is very tender and soft. Stir in a little water if the mixture starts to dry out. Remove the lamb from the oven and let stand for 10 minutes before carving.

To serve, cut the lamb into 1 cm/½ inch slices. Place the shin bone on a serving platter and arrange the slices over and around the bone; place a frill on the tip of the bone. Flame the brandy in a small saucepan, then strain the cooking juices into it. Stir in the cream and simmer for 1 minute. Pour this sauce over the lamb slices and serve at once garnished with onion slices and lemon wedges.

PREVIOUS SPREAD, clockwise from bottom left: Rogan Josh (*page 102*); Raan (*page 106*); Mint and Yogurt Chutney (*page 44*); Gosht Pasanda (*page 103*); Raita (*page 126*); Murgh Biryani (*page 107*); Tadka Dal (*page 126*).

MURGH BIRYANI
Chicken with Spiced Rice

SEE PHOTOGRAPH ON PAGE 105

THIS IS A COMBINATION of curried chicken and aromatic rice, partially cooked separately and then steamed together. It's like an explosion when you open the lid. It's not a difficult dish to make, but it has to be very precisely made to get the rice and chicken just right. You can make in smaller quantities, but I think this is ideal for family celebrations or gatherings.

SERVES 8

900 g/2 lb/4½ cups basmati rice

2 chickens, each about 1.5 kg/3½ lb, skinned, boned and cut into 2.5 cm/
1 inch cubes

350 ml/12 fl oz/1½ cups natural yogurt (page 33)

1 tablespoon ground coriander

1 tablespoon Kashmiri red chilli powder or cayenne pepper

2 teaspoons turmeric   salt, to taste

3 tablespoons vegetable oil

4 onions, sliced

1½ tablespoons Ginger and Garlic Paste (page 29)

4 tomatoes, cubed

6 green chillies, seeded and thinly sliced lengthways

2.5 cm/1 inch piece of fresh root ginger, peeled and cut into julienne sticks

½ bunch fresh coriander/cilantro leaves, chopped

2 tablespoons garam masala

1 teaspoon saffron   1 sprig fresh mint

25 g/1 oz/2 tablespoons ghee

1 teaspoon cumin seeds

225 ml/8 fl oz/1 cup milk

chopped fresh coriander/cilantro leaves, to garnish

WASH THE RICE by putting it in a large bowl and covering with water, then stir and drain off the cloudy water. Repeat 3 or 4 times until the water remains clear. Cover with fresh water and leave to soak for 30 minutes. Meanwhile, place the chicken in a glass bowl. Add the yogurt, ground coriander, chilli powder, turmeric and salt and marinate for 20 minutes.

Heat the oil in a large flameproof casserole with a tight-fitting lid. Add half the onions and fry until golden brown. Remove with a slotted spoon and drain on crumpled kitchen paper/paper towels; set aside for the garnish. Add the rest of the onions to the casserole and fry until light brown. Stir in the ginger and garlic paste and fry until the aroma of fried garlic is evident. Stir in the chicken pieces with the marinade and simmer, stirring occasionally, until the mixture becomes

watery. Add the tomatoes, cover and simmer for 18–20 minutes until the chicken is cooked through and tender.

Remove the casserole from the heat and stir in the sliced green chilli, ginger, coriander/cilantro, garam masala, ½ teaspoon of the saffron and half the browned onions; cover and set aside. Meanwhile, bring a large saucepan of water, about 3 times the volume of the rice, to the boil. Add the mint, ghee, cumin seeds and salt and return to the boil. Add the drained rice and boil/simmer for 4–5 minutes until half cooked. Drain well. Place the rice on top of the chicken mixture. Sprinkle the remaining saffron over and pour in the milk. Cover with a wet towel, then a lid and cook in an oven preheated to 200°–220°C/400°–425°F/Gas 6–7 for 18–20 minutes. To serve, loosen the rice in the pan with a fork. Garnish with the reserved brown onions and coriander.

Red Chillies
on Green Cardamom Pods

Some like it Hot

FRESH GREEN CHILLIS. Dry red chillis. Black pepper. Cinnamon, cloves, cardomom and mace. I always argue that Indian food is to do with spices, not chillis. After all, India, and especially Bombay, was at the centre of the spice trade – at different times, different traders would come through and bring different spices, which were planted and gradually naturalized. Even the chilli itself is not indigenous to India. It's a plant introduced from South America by the Portuguese in the 1600s. In fact, early accounts of food in Bombay from the first British people there make no mention of the dishes being hot, because they almost certainly weren't – just spicy.

But there is something addictive about the chilli. I can still vividly remember my college days when my friends and I would take a bus down to Bandra Station in Bombay and dig into large portions of *Sukha Tikha Mutton* (dry and hot mutton) and *Dal Fry* at the National Dhaba. We needed big mugs of beer to wash down the food and cool our perspiring bodies. This weekly ritual left us feeling great. Nevertheless,

even I was amazed, when I first came to England at how hot some British diners took their food. It was more than I could handle!

The chilli is used differently in cooking throughout the sub-continent. Kashmiri food can be fiery, reflecting the hot Kashmiri chilli. We leave the seeds out of these when we grind them! In North India, Western India and Goa, they use red chillis in dried form. Central India has a heritage of using exotic spices in a more balanced way. Eastern India with its rich culture of Bengali food has an abundance of green chillis and ground mustard to boost its spice levels. Southern India relies on the crushed black pepper and red chilli combination to get the sweat pores open.

Many of the recipes in this book use chilli. But these recipes are really hot. You can't grade curry on the *korma-madras-vindaloo* scale so popular in high-street Indian restaurants, where they simply add more raw chilli for each level. We look for a mellower, cooked heat, not just on your palate but through your whole system.

MIRCHI KORMA
Kashmiri-Style Lamb with Red Chilli

SEE PHOTOGRAPH ON PAGE 112

A HOT *KORMA*? Yes! Although in everyday curry-house language a *'korma'* means mild, it's a misconception. In reality the word refers to the style of cooking – slowly simmering all the ingredients together. You should be able to find Kashmiri chilli powder in Indian stores, but if it isn't available substitute cayenne pepper.

SERVES 4

2 tablespoons vegetable oil
6 cloves
1 tablespoon Ginger and Garlic Paste (page 29)
900 g/2 lb leg of lamb, cubed and rinsed
750 g/1½ lb tomatoes, chopped, puréed and strained
2 tablespoons lemon juice
salt, to taste
8 fried green chillies, to garnish

FOR THE MASALA
100 g/4 oz dry red chillies, or 5 tablespoons Kashmiri red chilli powder or cayenne pepper
6 green cardamom pods
4 cloves
3 pieces of mace
2 tablespoons Fried Brown Onions (page 32)
1 tablespoon coriander seeds
½ tablespoon Schezwan peppers
½ tablespoon cumin seeds
2 teaspoons turmeric
1 teaspoon black peppercorns

TO MAKE THE MASALA, place all the ingredients in a blender or food processor and process until a fine paste forms. Add a little warm water if necessary. Heat the oil in a large flame-proof casserole or wok. Add the cloves and ginger and garlic paste and fry them until the aroma of cooked garlic is evident. Stir in the masala paste and cook for 5–6 minutes, stirring occasionally.

Add the lamb and simmer for about 20 minutes, stirring occasionally, until it is half cooked. Add the tomatoes and continue simmering about a further 20 minutes until the lamb is cooked through and tender. The consistency should be quite thin, so stir in warm water as necessary while the curry cooks. Season with the lemon juice and salt. Serve garnished with fried green chillies.

GOSHT CHETTINAD
Lamb Cooked in the Chettiyar House Style
SEE PHOTOGRAPH ON PAGE 111

DOWN IN SOUTHERN INDIA, in Tamil Nadu, is the home of the Chettiyars, a famous Indian landlord dynasty with a well-known tradition of fine cooking. This a typical recipe from a Chettiyar chef. If you don't have a fresh coconut, use 50 g/2 oz/½ cup desiccated/shredded coconut.

SERVES 4

1 tablespoon vegetable oil

1 large onion, finely sliced

1 teaspoon turmeric

salt, to taste

900 g/2 lb boneless leg of lamb, cubed

1 tablespoon tamarind pulp (page 33)

chopped fresh coriander/cilantro leaves, to garnish

FOR THE MASALA

¼ fresh coconut, peeled and grated (see Introduction)

8 black peppercorns

8 dried red chillies

6 garlic cloves

3 black cardamom pods, cracked

2 cloves

1 cm/½ inch piece of cinnamon stick

1 tablespoon coriander seeds

1 tablespoon poppy seeds

1 teaspoon cumin seeds

¼ teaspoon brown mustard seeds

TO MAKE THE MASALA, roast all the ingredients in a dry frying pan/skillet or wok until the aromas begin to waft up. Transfer to an electric spice mill and process until a fine powder forms; set aside. Heat the oil in a large flameproof casserole with a tight-fitting lid. Add the onion and fry until it turns golden brown. Stir in the ground masala, turmeric and salt. Add the lamb and fry for about 20 minutes, stirring occasionally, until it is golden and all the natural juices it will give off start to dry up. Pour in enough water to cover the lamb, cover the pan and simmer until the lamb is almost tender. Add the tamarind pulp and salt and continue simmering for 30–35 minutes until the lamb is tender. The gravy for this dish should have a coating consistency and should not be too runny. Serve garnished with coriander/cilantro.

KORI GASI

Thin Chicken Curry with Coconut Milk

FROM KERALA, this curry is fiery hot and best eaten with plain boiled rice. If you cannot get fresh coconut, substitute 225 g/ 8 oz/2 cups desiccated/shredded coconut, but there will be a marginal difference in taste.

SERVES 4

2 fresh coconuts, grated (see Introduction)

1 tablespoon vegetable oil

1 onion, sliced

18–20 dried red chillies   6 garlic cloves, sliced

2 tablespoons coriander seeds

1 teaspoon cumin seeds

1 teaspoon black peppercorns

½ teaspoon fenugreek seeds

½ teaspoon turmeric

15 g/½ oz/1 tablespoon salted butter

1 chicken, about 1.5 kg/3½ lb, skinned, boned and cut into 4 cm/1½ inch cubes

juice of 1 lemon

FOR THE TEMPERING

1 tablespoon vegetable oil

1 onion, finely chopped

1 teaspoon Garam Masala (page 28)

USE THE GRATED FLESH of 1½ of the coconuts to make 450 ml/16 fl oz/2 cups thick coconut milk and 450 ml/16 fl oz/ 2 cups thin coconut milk (page 32). Dry-roast the remaining grated coconut flesh until it is brown in colour; remove from the pan and set aside. Heat the oil in a large saucepan. Add the onion and fry until it is brown. Add the chillies, garlic, coriander and cumin seeds, peppercorns, fenugreek seeds and turmeric and stir-fry for 3–4 minutes until a strong aroma of fried spices wafts up.

Transfer the spices with a slotted spoon to a blender or food processor. Add the browned coconut and thin coconut milk and blend to make a smooth masala paste. Melt the butter in a large saucepan or flameproof casserole. Add the masala paste and bring to the boil. Add the chicken, thick coconut milk and lemon juice, cover and simmer for about 30 minutes until the chicken is cooked through and tender. This is supposed to be a thin curry, so add a little water if necessary. To make the tempering, heat the oil in a small frying pan/skillet. Add the onions and fry until brown. Add the garam masala and swirl it around in the pan. Pour over the curry, then re-cover the pan for 5 minutes. Serve hot.

PREVIOUS SPREAD, clockwise from top centre: Mirchi Korma (*page 110*); Roti (*page 71*) and Laccha Paratha (*page 72*); Jheenga Tawa Masala (*page 115*); Masala Bhaat (*page 90*); Gosht Chettinad (*page 111*).

JHEENGA TAWA MASALA
Prawns in Masala Cooked on a Flat Griddle

SEE PHOTOGRAPH ON PAGE 113

THIS IS A DISH that's traditionally quickly stir-fried on a *tawa*, or flat griddle, but if you don't have one use a frying pan/skillet. It's a Punjabi dish that you would expect to find at a roadside stall in Bombay, very fresh and very quickly served. The makhani gravy in this dish is useful for cooking most meat, fish or vegetables in. It can be made up to four days in advance and kept in a covered container in the refrigerator.

SERVES 4

1 kg/2¼ lb raw prawns, peeled, deveined and rinsed

juice of 1 lemon

salt, to taste

2 tablespoons Ginger and Garlic Paste (page 29)

2 tablespoons vegetable oil

150 g/5 oz/1 cup onions, chopped

6 green chillies, seeded and chopped

4 teaspoons finely chopped peeled fresh root ginger

1 tablespoon black peppercorns, crushed

1 teaspoon garam masala (page 28)

2 tablespoons chopped fresh coriander/cilantro

freshly baked Naan (page 69) or bread rolls, to serve

FOR THE MAKHANI GRAVY

750 g/1½ lb tomatoes, chopped

4 green cardamom pods   3 green chillies, chopped

6 garlic cloves

4 cm/1½ inch piece of fresh root ginger, peeled and chopped

2 teaspoons Kashmiri red chilli powder or cayenne pepper

1 tablespoon tomato purée/paste

45 g/1½ oz/3 tablespoons butter

45 ml/1½ fl oz/3 tablespoons double/heavy cream

½ tablespoon sugar   2 teaspoons ground white pepper

2 teaspoons ground dried fenugreek leaves

salt, to taste

TO MAKE THE MAKHANI GRAVY, place the tomatoes, cardamom pods, chillies, cloves, ginger and chilli powder into a large saucepan or wok and bring to the boil. Lower the heat and simmer, uncovered, for about 2 hours, stirring occasionally. Transfer to a blender or food processor and purée, working in batches if necessary, then strain. Return to the pan, add the tomato purée/paste and bring to the simmer. Add the butter, cream, sugar, white pepper, ground fenugreek leaves and salt; set aside.

Place the prawns in a glass bowl and sprinkle with the lemon juice and salt. Combine the ginger and garlic paste, oil and salt and rub all over the shrimp. Cover and leave to marinate for 15 minutes. Heat the oil in a large *tawa* or frying pan/skillet. Add the prawns, along with their marinade and stir-fry for 3–4 minutes until they turn pink and curl. Push the shrimp to the side of the pan. Add the onions, chillies, ginger and peppercorns and continue stir-frying for one minute. Return the shrimp to the centre of the pan and continue stir-frying for 2 minutes. Add the makhani gravy and stir until well blended. Sprinkle with the garam masala and coriander/cilantro and stir together. Serve at once with naans or bread rolls.

Raw Mangoes
and Drum Sticks
on Yellow Lentils

Vegetarian Dishes

VEGETABLES ABOUND IN EVERY FORM IN INDIA. The majority of Indians are Hindus and a large percentage – though not all – are vegetarians. Also, on a certain day every week even a meat-eating Hindu will be vegetarian – the day depends on which deity or goddess you worship. Vegetarian food is simple and not heavily spiced – perhaps spinach stir-fried with garlic and cumin, or in South India, a lentil purée with gourd. In Bihar or Uttar Pradesh, every meal has some kind of stir-fried vegetable. Even in Bengal the meal starts with a vegetable dish in fried form, or some sort of light stew, before you go on to the meat. In India, a vegetable is typically washed, cut and stir-fried first, before a little water is added and it is simmered.

Lentils are an excellent source of protein and are cooked all over India in different guises – *sambar* in the south, *mori dal* in Gujerat where the yellow lentil is puréed and tempered very lightly. In Bengal you have *cholar dal*, Bengal gram boiled and tempered with chillis, sugar and maybe coconut. In the north, *dal makhani* is black lentils with kidney beans, simmered overnight and enriched with butter and cream. All over India, *dal* is an essential part of the menu, and in the Bombay melting pot you'll find it in every form.

Most Indians have three vegetables when they are eating a meal at home – typically a green vegetable, a potato dish and a lentil dish. That's what we serve with our main dishes at the Brasserie. In England and the USA, you should be able to find almost all of the vegetables available to Indian cooks, not imported from India but from Africa. I have seen even the red-leaved *sag* in street markets in east London. Even the large superstores sell a lot of Indian vegetables. The most typical ones are *dudhi* (bottle gourd), *karela* (bitter gourd), *turai* (ridge gourd), *parwal* (snake gourd), *methi* (fenugreek leaves) and *suran* (yam). All these vegetables are quite dear and kilo for kilo almost compare to the price of fresh lamb.

Incidentally, you must make sure you wash your vegetables before you cut them, to preserve the nutrients. The cooking time should be minimum in all cases – keep them nice and crunchy.

SABUT ALOO KI BHAJI ⓥ
Whole Unpeeled Potatoes with Tempering

SEE PHOTOGRAPH ON PAGE 124

THESE ARE BOILED and fried whole small new potatoes that are then tossed with curry leaves and spices.

SERVES 4

450 g/1 lb/3 cups unskinned new potatoes, par-boiled

vegetable oil for deep-frying, plus extra for pan-frying

½ teaspoon mustard seeds

6 curry leaves, optional

2 small onions, sliced

½ teaspoon ground asafoetida

3 green chillies, chopped

2 tomatoes, cubed

2.5 cm/1 inch piece of fresh root ginger, peeled and chopped

1½ teaspoons turmeric

juice of ½ lemon

salt, to taste

1 tablespoon chopped fresh coriander/cilantro leaves, to garnish

HEAT ENOUGH OIL to fry the potatoes in a deep saucepan to 220°C/425°F, or until a cube of bread browns in about 30 seconds. Add the potatoes, in batches if necessary, and deep-fry until the skins are golden brown and crisp.

Heat 1 tablespoon oil in a large frying pan/skillet or wok. Add the mustard seeds and stir until they start to crackle. Add the curry leaves, onions and asafoetida and stir-fry until the onions soften. Stir in the chillies, tomatoes, ginger and turmeric and continue stir-frying until they are warmed through. Add the potatoes, lemon juice and salt and stir together. Garnish with the coriander/cilantro and serve.

VEGETABLE PORIAL ⓥ
Stir-Fried Vegetables

FROM SOUTHERN INDIA, using the day's fresh vegetables – cabbage, beans, carrots – all nice and crunchy.

SERVES 4

1 tablespoon vegetable oil

1 teaspoon yellow split peas

1½ teaspoons brown mustard seeds

8–10 curry leaves, optional

1 teaspoon chopped peeled fresh root ginger

1 teaspoon chopped green chilli

200 g/7 oz/heaped 2 cups cabbage, diced

150 g/5 oz/1½ cups thin green beans, diced

200 g/7 oz/1¾ cups carrots, grated

100 g/4 oz/1 cup fresh coconut, grated

salt, to taste

chopped fresh coriander/cilantro leaves, to garnish

HEAT THE OIL in a large frying pan/skillet or wok. Add the yellow split peas and mustard seeds and fry until they crackle. Stir in the curry leaves, then add the ginger and chilli and stir-fry for 2–3 minutes. Add the cabbage, beans and carrots and quickly stir-fry until heated through. Add the coconut and salt and continue stir-frying until the vegetables are cooked through but still crisp. Serve garnished with the coriander/cilantro.

MAKKI-KHUMB MASALA Ⓥ
Corn and Mushrooms in Gravy

KHUMB is one of the many terms in India for mushrooms, and here it translates into button mushrooms.

SERVES 4

2 tablespoons vegetable oil

2 small onions, chopped

4 green chillies, chopped

4 cm/1½ inch piece of fresh root ginger, peeled and chopped

2 tablespoons Ginger and Garlic Paste (page 29)

2 teaspoons Kashmiri red chilli powder or cayenne pepper

5 small tomatoes, chopped

450 g/1 lb button mushrooms, trimmed

250 g/9 oz baby corn cut into 1 cm/½ inch pieces

1 small red pepper, cored, seeded and diced

1 small green pepper, cored, seeded and diced

1 large tomato, diced

salt, to taste

2 teaspoons garam masala (page 28)

chopped fresh coriander/cilantro leaves, to garnish

HEAT THE OIL in a saucepan. Add the onions and fry, stirring often, until golden brown. Stir in the chillies, ginger, ginger and garlic paste and chilli powder and stir-fry until the aroma of cooked garlic is evident. Stir in a little water if the mixture is too thick. Add the chopped tomatoes and continue stirring until the fat separates. Add the mushrooms and corn and continue stir-frying for 2 minutes. Stir in the peppers and diced tomato. Adjust the seasoning and sprinkle with garam masala. Serve garnished with the coriander/cilantro.

KAJU AUR MUTTAR CURRY Ⓥ
Cashew and Green Pea Curry

THIS DISH is very popular with vegetarians in India, particularly Gujeratis. It make an ideal supplement at wedding banquets at the Brasserie.

SERVES 4

250 g/9 oz/1⅔ cups shelled cashew nuts

2 tablespoons vegetable oil, plus extra for deep-frying the nuts

2 teaspoons cumin seeds

2 onions, sliced

0.5 cm/¼ inch piece of fresh root ginger, peeled and chopped

1 teaspoon turmeric

4 teaspoons Kashmiri red chilli powder or cayenne pepper

2½ tablespoons Garlic Paste (page 29)

150 g/5 oz/⅔ cup tomatoes, chopped

250 g/9 oz/1⅔ cups shelled green peas, par-boiled

salt to taste

2 tablespoons chopped fresh coriander/cilantro leaves, plus extra to garnish

HEAT ENOUGH OIL to fry the cashew nuts in a saucepan to 180°C/350°F, or until a cube of bread browns in 45 seconds. Add the nuts and fry until golden brown. Remove with a slotted spoon and drain well on crumpled kitchen paper/paper towels; set aside. Heat 2 tablespoons oil in a large frying pan/skillet. Add the cumin seeds and fry until they crackle. Stir in the onion and stir-fry until it is golden brown. Add the ginger and turmeric and continue frying for 1 minute. Add the chilli powder and garlic paste and continue simmering until the fat separates.

Add a little water and continue to simmer until the mixture is dry. Repeat this process twice; the gravy should be thick. Add the tomatoes and continue simmering until they break down and blend into the gravy. Add a little water to adjust the consistency if necessary. Stir in the cashews and peas and continue simmering until the peas are cooked through. Add salt. Stir in the coriander/cilantro. Serve garnished with extra coriander.

BHARELI TAMATAR Ⓥ
Stuffed Tomatoes

SEE PHOTOGRAPH ON PAGE 125

BE SURE to use large, ripe tomatoes for this. Stuffed with potatoes, these make a filling side dish.

MAKES 8

4 potatoes

1 tablespoon grated paneer

8 tomatoes

1 tablespoon vegetable oil

1 tablespoon cumin seeds

1 tablespoon chopped fresh coriander/cilantro leaves

2 teaspoons crushed peanuts

1 teaspoon chopped green chilli

1 teaspoon Kashmiri red chilli powder or cayenne pepper

½ teaspoon chopped peeled fresh root ginger

pinch of sugar

salt, to taste

BRING A LARGE PAN of water to the boil. Add the potatoes and boil until they are tender. Drain well, and peel when cool enough to handle, then mash with the paneer; set aside. Meanwhile, slice the tops off the tomatoes and scoop out the centres with a spoon. Chop the flesh and reserve for the stuffing. Heat the oil in a large frying pan/skillet. Add the cumin, coriander/cilantro, peanuts, chilli, chilli powder, ginger, sugar and salt and stir together. Stir in the chopped tomato pulp and simmer for 2 minutes, stirring.

Pour the ingredients from the pan over the potatoes and stir together. Use this mixture to stuff the tomatoes. Place the tomatoes, open end down, on a baking sheet and cook in an oven preheated to 200°C/400°F/Gas 6 for 8–10 minutes until the tomatoes just yield when you squeeze them. Serve at once.

BHINDI JAIPURI Ⓥ
Crisply Fried Okra and Onions

SEE PHOTOGRAPH ON PAGE 125

A DISH I ONCE HAD IN JAIPUR, in Rajastan, which I have recreated in London. Fried and savoury, this is actually more of an accompaniment than a vegetable side dish, and goes very well with *Rogan Josh* (page 102) and *Nisteachi Kodi* (page 90). It will keep for two or three days.

SERVES 4

900 g/2 lb okra, diagonally cut into julienne slices

2 onions, sliced

150 g/5 oz/1 cup gram flour

2 teaspoons turmeric

2 teaspoons Kashmiri red chilli powder or cayenne pepper

vegetable oil for deep-frying

1 teaspoon dry mango powder

1 tablespoon shop-bought chaat masala

salt, to taste

juice of ½ lemon

½ bunch fresh coriander/cilantro leaves, chopped, to garnish

PLACE THE OKRA and onions in a bowl. Stir in the gram flour, turmeric and chilli powder and mix together. Heat enough oil to fry the mixture to 180°C/350°F, or until a cube of bread browns in about 45 seconds in it. Pick up the okra and onions with your hand and drop handfuls into the oil and fry until golden brown. Remove with a slotted spoon and drain well on crumpled kitchen paper/paper towels. Do not fry too many at a time or the temperature will drop too much and the texture will not be crispy. Toss with the mango powder, chaat masala and salt. Sprinkle over the lemon juice and serve at once with the coriander/cilantro leaves sprinkled on top.

Turai (Ridge Gourds)
on Red Kidney Beans

BRINJAL KALWA Ⓥ
Aubergines/Eggplants, Gujerati Style

THIS IS A TYPICAL GUJERATI PREPARATION – the aubergines/eggplants are sliced and fried, then tossed in a special paste. They are hot and savoury with just a hint of sweetness.

SERVES 4

vegetable oil for deep-frying

1 kg/2¼ lb aubergines/eggplants, halved lengthwise and thinly sliced

2 tablespoons vegetable oil

6–8 curry leaves, optional   1 teaspoon cumin seeds

3 onions, sliced

100 g/4 oz/heaped ¾ cup gram flour

1 teaspoon Kashmiri red chilli powder or cayenne pepper

1 teaspoon turmeric

1 teaspoon ground coriander   1 teaspoon ground cumin

2 teaspoons jaggery or dark brown sugar, dissolved in 1 tablespoon water

2 tablespoons cashew nuts, chopped

1 teaspoon lemon juice

salt, to taste

chopped fresh coriander/cilantro leaves, to garnish

HEAT ENOUGH OIL to fry the aubergines/eggplants in a deep saucepan to 200°C/400°F, or until a cube of bread browns in about 30 seconds. Add the aubergine/eggplant slices, in batches, and fry until golden brown. Drain well on crumpled kitchen paper/paper towels.

Heat 2 tablespoons oil in a large saucepan or wok. Add the curry leaves and cumin seeds and fry until they crackle. Add the onions and fry, stirring occasionally, until they are golden brown. Reduce the heat and stir in the gram flour, chilli powder, turmeric, ground coriander and ground cumin and continue simmering until the mixture leaves the sides of the pan. Stir in the dissolved jaggery. Toss the aubergines and cashews in the mixture, then add the lemon juice and salt. Serve garnished with the chopped coriander/cilantro.

BAINGAN BHURTA Ⓥ
Mashed Aubergine/Eggplant

THIS IS A WONDERFUL WINTER DISH. In India aubergines/eggplants are a winter crop, and when homes were heated with coal fires in the northern parts of India housewives would economize by chargrilling different vegetables. It is particularly good with *Roti* (page 71) – the smoked flavour comes through beautifully.

SERVES 4

4 large aubergines/eggplants, about 900 g/2 lb total weight

1 tablespoon vegetable oil, plus a little extra for chargrilling

25 g/1 oz/2 tablespoons butter

5 green chillies, finely chopped

2 onions, finely chopped   2 garlic cloves, finely chopped

2.5 cm/1 inch piece of fresh root ginger, peeled and finely chopped

1 tablespoon turmeric

2 teaspoons chilli powder   5 tomatoes, finely chopped

1 tablespoon garam masala (page 28)

salt, to taste

chopped fresh coriander/cilantro, to garnish

BASTE THE AUBERGINES/eggplants with a small amount of the oil and chargrill until the skins are almost crisp. It is best to do this over coals on a barbecue, otherwise boil the aubergines for 20 minutes, then drain well. You can also cook them under a hot grill/broiler. When the aubergines are cool enough to handle, peel off the skins and mash the flesh.

Melt the butter with the remaining oil in a large flameproof casserole or wok. Add the chillies, onions, garlic and ginger and stir-fry until the onions are translucent. Add the turmeric and chilli powder and continue stir-frying for 3 minutes. Stir in the tomatoes and continue cooking for a further 2 minutes. Stir in the mashed aubergine pulp and stir-fry for 6 minutes. Add the garam masala and salt. Serve garnished with the coriander/cilantro.

ELUMICHAI SADAM Ⓥ
Lemon Rice

SEE PHOTOGRAPH ON PAGE 124

THIS STYLE OF COOKING RICE is typically South Indian, and a variety of extra ingredients can be added to produce a whole range of rice dishes. The best-known examples are coconut rice, tamarind rice and yogurt rice, to name a few. When you have leftover boiled rice, this is an ideal way to re-heat it the following day. Look for black lentils in Indian grocery shops labelled as *urad dal*, and the yellow gram labelled as *channa dal*.

SERVES 4

750 g/1½ lb/3¾ cups basmati rice

2 tablespoons vegetable oil

salt, to taste

1 tablespoon split and skinned black lentils or urad dal, *well rinsed and drained*

1 teaspoon fenugreek seeds

1 teaspoon turmeric

10 curry leaves, optional

½ teaspoon brown mustard seeds

pinch of ground asafoetida

1 tablespoon split yellow gram or channa dal, *well rinsed and drained*

20 shelled cashew nuts

6 dried red chillies, optional

WASH THE RICE by putting it in a large bowl and covering with water, then stir and drain off the cloudy water. Repeat 3 or 4 times until the water remains clear. Cover with fresh water and leave to soak for 30 minutes. Bring a large saucepan with water, about three times the volume of the rice, to the boil. Add 1 tablespoon of the oil and salt to the water, then stir in the drained rice. Cook for 12–15 minutes, stirring occasionally, until the rice grains are just cooked but still a bit firm. Drain well and spread out so the rice grains remain separate. When they are dry, transfer to a large glass bowl. Dry-roast the black lentils and fenugreek seeds in a frying pan/skillet for 3 minutes. Sprinkle over the turmeric, then transfer to an electric spice mill and process until finely ground. Sprinkle over the rice in the bowl.

Heat the remaining oil in the frying pan. Add, in sequence, the curry leaves, mustard seeds, asafoetida, yellow gram, cashews and chillies. Fry until golden brown and the aroma of fried spices wafts up. Pour this over the rice and mix together well. Re-heat the rice in a flameproof casserole with a tight-fitting lid in an oven preheated to 220°C/425°F/Gas 7 for 8–10 minutes before serving.

CUCUMBER RAITA Ⓥ
Cucumber and Yogurt

SEE PHOTOGRAPHS ON PAGES 105 AND 124

A *RAITA* HELPS NEUTRALIZE chillies and spices to clear the palate. Indians have many ways of preparing *raita*: in the South, they prefer the yogurt plain, while in central India it will be perked up with cumin and various vegetables.

SERVES 4

500 ml/18 fl oz/2½ cups natural yogurt (page 33)

½ teaspoon sugar

½ teaspoon ground cumin, plus extra for sprinkling

½ teaspoon Kashmiri red chilli powder or cayenne pepper, plus extra for sprinkling

salt, to taste

½ cucumber, grated

1 tablespoon chopped fresh coriander/cilantro

PLACE THE YOGURT in a bowl and whisk in the sugar, cumin, chilli powder and salt. Stir in the cucumber. Sprinkle with extra cumin and chilli powder and the coriander/cilantro. Chill to serve as an accompaniment.

PREVIOUS SPREAD, clockwise from bottom left: Elumichai Sadam (*page 123*); Pudina Paratha (*page 73*); Cucumber Raita (*page 126*); Sabut Aloo Ki Bhaji (*page 118*); Bhindi Jaipuri (*page 120*); Bhareli Tamatar (*page 120*); Dal Makhani (*page 127*).

TADKA DAL Ⓥ
Tempered Lentils

SEE PHOTOGRAPH ON PAGE 104

YOU CAN USE YELLOW OR RED LENTILS, or a combination of the two. *Tadka* means that after the lentils are boiled, they are tempered with a full-flavoured tempering.

SERVES 4 AS AN ACCOMPANIMENT

150 g/5 oz/1 cup yellow lentils, well rinsed and drained

75 g/3 oz/½ cup red lentils, well rinsed and drained

1½ teaspoons turmeric

salt, to taste

chopped fresh coriander/cilantro, to garnish

FOR THE TEMPERING

15 g/½ oz/1 tablespoon ghee

1 teaspoon cumin seeds   3 garlic cloves, sliced

pinch of ground asafoetida

1 onion, chopped   2 green chillies, chopped

0.5 cm/¼ inch piece of fresh root ginger, peeled and chopped

1 teaspoon Kashmiri red chilli powder or cayenne pepper

2 tomatoes, coarsely chopped

PUT 1.2 LITRES/2 PINTS/5 CUPS WATER in a large saucepan. Add the lentils, turmeric and salt and bring to the boil. Lower the heat and simmer, skimming the surface as necessary, until the lentils are soft and most of the liquid absorbed. Whisk them until they form a coarse paste with a pouring consistency that isn't too watery; set aside while preparing the tempering.

For the tempering, melt the ghee in a frying pan/skillet. Add the cumin seeds and fry until they crackle. Add the garlic and asafoetida and continue frying, stirring occasionally, until the aroma of cooked garlic is evident. Add the onion and continue frying until it turns brown. Stir the green chillies, ginger and chilli powder and continue frying for 1½ minutes. Stir in the tomatoes. Pour the tempering ingredients over the lentils and stir together. Serve garnished with coriander/cilantro.

DAL MAKHANI Ⓥ
Stewed Pulses/Legumes with Butter and Cream

SEE PHOTOGRAPH ON PAGE 124

BLACK LENTILS with their skin on gives a gel effect to this slowly cooked dish. The easiest way to prepare all the spices is to put them in a muslin/cheesecloth bag that can be removed after cooking.

SERVES 4 AS AN ACCOMPANIMENT

150 g/5 oz/1 cup black lentils or urad dal, *with their skins left on, well rinsed and drained*

75 g/3 oz/½ cup yellow split gram or channa dal, *well rinsed and drained*

75 g/3 oz/½ cup dried red kidney beans, *boiled for 10 minutes, well rinsed and drained*

6 green cardamom pods

4 cloves   3 dried bay leaves

2 garlic cloves, peeled   2 black cardamom pods

2.5 cm/1 inch piece of cinnamon stick

0.5 cm/¼ inch piece of fresh root ginger, peeled and grated

2 teaspoons coriander seeds

1 onion, sliced

25 g/1 oz/2 tablespoons butter

2 tablespoons single/light cream

salt, to taste

chopped fresh coriander/cilantro leaves, to garnish

FOR THE TEMPERING

1 tablespoon vegetable oil

1 teaspoon cumin seeds

2 garlic cloves, sliced

1 small onion, finely chopped

2 whole green chillies

2 teaspoons Kashmiri red chilli powder or cayenne pepper

1 teaspoon turmeric

100 ml/4 fl oz/½ cup tomato juice

SOAK THE PULSES/legumes in water to cover for 1 hour. Meanwhile, tie the green cardamoms, cloves, bay leaves, garlic, black cardamoms, cinnamon, ginger and coriander seeds in a large piece of muslin/cheesecloth, as if making a bouquet garni. Drain the pulses and put them in a deep saucepan with double their volume of water. Add the onion and spice bag and bring to the boil. Lower the heat and simmer, skimming the surface as necessary, until all the pulses are soft, which can take up to 2 hours; top up with additional water as necessary. Use a wooden spoon to stir and mash the lentils as they cook: aim for a thick mash without any whole grains. Stir in the butter and all but 1 teaspoon of the cream and keep simmering while you prepare the tempering.

For the tempering, heat the oil in a small frying pan/skillet. Add the cumin and fry until the seeds crackle and turn brown. Add the garlic and when slices start to turn brown, stir in the onion and continue frying until it turns brown. Stir in the chillies, chilli powder, turmeric and tomato juice and simmer for 2 minutes. Pour the tempering over the *dal* and add salt. Stir together well and simmer for 2 minutes. Swirl with the reserved cream and serve garnished with coriander/cilantro.

Bell Gourds
and Bay Leaves
on Green Mung Beans

Specialities of The Bombay Brasserie

T HE BOMBAY BRASSERIE is famous for its house specialities, often served at buffets and banquets or specially ordered by long-term regulars. The influences for these are spread right across the sub-continent. While working for the Taj Group based in Bombay, I was lucky enough to travel all over India to more than 30 hotels in different parts of the country. Everywhere I went, I watched and documented the cooking, to be tried out when I returned to Bombay. Sometimes it was food cooked in the hotel, sometimes a speciality at a local restaurant, sometimes something traditional prepared at the house of one of the chefs, usually by their wife or mother: they would often let me watch in the kitchen and ask questions. I've still got my old notebooks, with marks out of ten for the recipes! I'm a great believer in eating out regularly, whether it's a basic place – what we in India call *dhabas*,

where the food is just plonked on the table – or the latest fashionable eaterie.

There is a surprising amount of creative leeway in Indian food. Unlike in the West, the classical traditions of Indian cookery were not often written down because the great cooks were not really literate. We never had our Mrs Beetons or Escoffiers. Each chef would have a slightly different way of doing a dish. The basic technique might be hard and fast – a *korma*, a *biryani* – but what goes in to the dish varies. One chef might use mint in his *biryani*, another might not use even a pinch. Every chef prides himself on having his own garam masala. I have six good but marginally different recipes for *Rogan Josh*.

Different restaurants have their specialities, too. In Calcutta, for example, there's an old one called Nizam where

I used to eat as a hard-up student. Their Nizam meat roll is still very popular and synonymous with the place. The recipe for Andhra Chicken comes from a restaurant in Andhra Pradesh called Anarkali, where it was known as Chicken Sixer. As I gathered up my recipes, I would return to Bombay and try them out. Standardizing recipes is very difficult in India. Housewives use hand measures and even restaurant chefs rarely use spoons, so everything is a handful of this, a pinch of that. I found that it is essential to taste the dish after you see it being prepared, so that you can correlate what you saw going in to what you are tasting.

All these dishes have been part of the Bombay Brasserie repertoire at one time or another. Some are my own ideas – like *Bhindi Jaipuri* in the vegetarian dishes section– and some are drawn from the cooking of my family and friends. Statistically, the specialities are our biggest-selling dishes. But statistics are for records. What is rewarding are the small hand-written notes of praise for the dishes left by our guests.

SHORSHE BATA MAACH
Fish with Mustard Paste

IN MY PART OF INDIA, Bengal and Bihar, we prepared this dish using *hilsa*, a fish which is similar to herring and has a lot of bones. It has a very distinctive smell, too, which lingers on your palate for some time – nevertheless, it one of the most-prized fishes in Bengal. The charm of this dish is its simplicity – freshly ground mustard with chillies, the fish fried nice and crisp and then quickly simmered in the sauce. It's mouth-watering, but it may give you a runny nose and eyes from the potent mustard.

SERVES 4

8 fish steaks or darnes of your choice, such as grey mullet, grass carp or

monkfish tails

1 tablespoon turmeric

salt

4 tablespoons yellow mustard seeds   4 green chillies, chopped

3 tablespoons mustard or vegetable oil

1 teaspoon black onion seeds   2 green chillies, slit

salt, to taste

PLACE THE FISH in a single layer in a glass dish and marinate in the turmeric and salt; set aside for 20 minutes. Meanwhile, soak the mustard seeds in 225 ml/8 fl oz/1 cup water for 10 minutes. Transfer the seeds and liquid to an electric blender or a pestle, add the chopped chillies and grind to a fine paste; set aside. Heat the oil in a *kadai* or wok; if you use mustard oil, heat it to smoking point and reduce it before you add the fish. Add the fish, in batches, and fry for 5–6 minutes until crisp and brown on the outside. Remove and set aside.

Strain the oil through a fine sieve/strainer into a large saucepan. Add the onion seeds and fry for about 45 seconds until they become crisp. Add the mustard seed paste and about 450 ml/16 fl oz/2 cups water and simmer for 10–12 minutes, stirring occasionally. Return the fish to the pan, in a single layer if possible, and add the slit chillies and enough water to cover. Cover and simmer for 3–4 minutes until warmed through and the flesh flakes easily if tested with the tip of a knife. Adjust the salt if necessary and serve at once.

LAU CHINGRI
Prawns/Shrimp with Bottle Gourd, Bengali Style

THIS IS A WONDERFUL MELANGE of a vegetable and seafood. Bottle gourd, or *doodi*, is a firm vegetable and it is simmered until tender to match the texture of the prawns/shrimp. If it isn't available, you can use a marrow/English marrow, but the results won't be exactly the same. The best I have eaten is my mum's, and I was taught this recipe by her.

SERVES 4

900 g/2 lb raw medium prawns/shrimp, shelled and deveined

2 teaspoons turmeric

½ teaspoon ajwain seeds

salt, to taste

3 tablespoons mustard or vegetable oil

2 dried bay leaves

1 teaspoon Panch Phoran (see page 33)

750 g/1½ lb bottle gourd, peeled and cut into small dice – use the soft core if the seeds are tender

4 green chillies, slit

1 tablespoon Kashmiri red chilli powder or cayenne pepper

1 teaspoon ground cumin

chopped fresh coriander/cilantro leaves, to garnish

PLACE THE PRAWNS/SHRIMP in a glass bowl with 1 teaspoon of the turmeric, the ajwain and salt and leave to marinate for about 20 minutes. Heat the oil in a flameproof casserole; if using mustard oil, heat it to the smoking point then let it cool down before adding the prawns. Add the prawns and fry for 4–5 minutes until they are crisp on the outside and curl.

Remove from the oil with a slotted spoon and drain well on crumpled kitchen paper/paper towels.

Re-heat the oil. Add the bay leaves and panch phoran and fry until the mustard seeds crackle. Add the bottle gourd and 225 ml/8 fl oz/1 cup water, cover and simmer for about 20 minutes until the gourd is tender; add extra water if necessary. Stir in the remaining turmeric, the chillies, chilli powder and ground cumin, re-cover and simmer for a further 3–4 minutes. Add the prawns and 225 ml/8 fl oz/1 cup water and simmer, stirring occasionally, for 6–7 minutes. Adjust the seasoning if necessary and serve, garnished with coriander/cilantro.

KARWARI JHINGA
Fried Prawns, Karwari Style
SEE PHOTOGRAPH ON PAGE 137

THE COASTAL STRETCH of Karwar is well known for its food. Karwari cooks are very sought after by Bombay restaurateurs, as their food is so well appreciated. I learned this recipe in Bombay from a young Karwari cook, who had learnt it from his mother.

SERVES 4

12 raw tiger prawns (or jumbo shrimp), deveined and butterflied
1 tablespoon tamarind pulp (page 33)
2 teaspoons red chilli powder
2 teaspoons Garlic Paste (page 29)
1 teaspoon turmeric
1 teaspoon ground cumin
salt, to taste
4 tablespoons coarse semolina
1 tablespoon rice flour
6 tablespoons vegetable oil for frying
lemon slices, to accompany

FOR THE CHUTNEY
100 g/4 oz/1 cup fresh coconut flesh, grated, or 25 g/1 oz/¼ cup desiccated/shredded coconut soaked in 100 ml/4 fl oz/½ cup water for 10 minutes
1 tablespoon Garlic Paste (page 29)
1 tablespoon tamarind pulp (page 33)
1 tablespoon Kashmiri red chilli powder or cayenne pepper
1 teaspoon turmeric
1 tablespoon vegetable oil
1½ teaspoons brown mustard seeds
8 curry leaves, chopped, optional

PLACE THE PRAWNS/SHRIMP in a glass bowl. Mix together the tamarind pulp, chilli powder, garlic paste, turmeric, cumin and salt. Pat on to the prawns, then set aside to marinate for 20 minutes. Meanwhile, make the chutney. Place the coconut, garlic paste, tamarind, chilli powder and turmeric into a blender or food processor and process until coarsely ground.

Heat the oil in a ladle. Add the mustard seeds and curry leaves and fry until they crackle. Pour this over the coconut mixture. Add salt and stir. Transfer to a small bowl to serve with the prawns. Mix the semolina and rice flour together, then coat the prawns with this mixture. Heat the oil until it is medium-hot. Add the prawns and fry until they are crisp and golden. Serve with lemon slices and the chutney.

BHAPA MAACH
Smoked Fish

BHAPA MEANS 'STEAMED', but this recipe actually involves steaming and smoking. This dish is a Mog recipe, and Mog cooks were the pioneers of blending Indian and Western cuisines. Use pine or hickory wood chips or sawdust.

SERVES 6

900 g/2 lb fresh herring, filleted with skin left on
juice of 1 lemon
juice of 1 small onion (flesh puréed and squeezed)
2 teaspoons ginger juice (flesh scraped and squeezed)
½ teaspoon sugar, plus an extra 3 tablespoons for smoking
salt, to taste
1 quantity potato straws (see Introduction, page 76), to serve

CUT THE HERRING FILLETS into manageable pieces and place in a glass bowl. Add the lemon juice, onion juice, ginger juice, ½ teaspoon sugar and salt. Stir together and leave to marinate for at least 30 minutes at room temperature. Use a smoker or a barbecue with an up-turned wok to cover the fish and hold in the smoke. Light the coals and cover with 225 g/8 oz wood chips or sawdust and the 3 tablespoons sugar. Cover with a wire mesh and place the fish on top. Close the lid or cover and cook for 9–10 minutes, or until one side is brown. Turn over and repeat on the other side.

Remove the fillets from the mesh and immediately place the flat side of a knife horizontally on them and press down. Use tweezers to remove the small bones as they stick out, like taking the small bones out of a salmon fillet. Cut into small fingers and serve with straw potatoes.

TALA MASALA MACCHI
Masala Fried Fish

THIS IS A POPULAR in-between-meals snack in Bombay, and likewise a great favourite here at the Bombay Brasserie – not only with the guests, but also with the staff. It is best to use boned and skinned large fish, such as cod or halibut. In India, *rawas* and *bhetki* are ideal.

SERVES 4

400 g/14 oz white fish fillets, skinned and cut into 2.5 cm/1 inch cubes
1 tablespoon Ginger and Garlic Paste (page 29)
2 tablespoons lemon juice
1 tablespoon Kashmiri red chilli powder or cayenne pepper
1 teaspoon chopped green chilli
1 teaspoon turmeric
1 teaspoon ground cumin
salt, to taste
200 g/7 oz/1¾ cups coarse semolina
100 g/4 oz/1 cup rice flour
vegetable oil for deep-frying
1 large onion, sliced, to garnish
chopped fresh coriander/cilantro leaves, to garnish

PLACE THE FISH in a glass bowl. Mix together the ginger and garlic paste, lemon juice, chilli powder, chilli, turmeric, cumin and salt. Pour over the fish and leave to marinate for 30 minutes. Mix together the semolina and rice flour. Coat the fish pieces with this mixture.

Heat the oil to 180°C/350°F, or until a cube of bread browns in about 45 seconds. Fry the fish, in batches if necessary, until golden brown. Drain well on crumpled kitchen paper/paper towels. Serve hot, garnished with onion slices and chopped coriander/cilantro.

KADAI MURG
Spiced Chicken Cooked in an Indian Wok

THIS DISH GETS ITS NAME from the Indian-style wok it is cooked in, a *kaдai*. This style of cooking involves quickly stir-frying the masala and then simmering the meat. It is a quick way of preparing a spicy dish when you are entertaining. This recipe is a typical north-western dish, and I was taught this by a Punjabi cook, who is now in Pakistan.

SERVES 4

8 dried red chillies

2 teaspoons coriander seeds   3 tablespoons vegetable oil

150 g/5 oz/1 cup onions, chopped

3½ teaspoons Garlic Paste (page 29)

1 teaspoon ajwain seeds   450 g/1 lb/3 cups tomatoes, chopped

6 green chillies, chopped

2 tablespoons chopped peeled fresh root ginger

1 tablespoon tomato purée/paste

1 chicken, about 1.5 kg/3½ lb, boned and cut into 2.5 cm/1 inch pieces

1 tablespoon lemon juice   1½ teaspoons dry fenugreek leaves

1 teaspoon garam masala (page 28)

salt, to taste

chopped fresh coriander/cilantro, to garnish

PLACE THE CHILLIES and coriander seeds in a dry frying pan/skillet and dry-roast until the aroma wafts up. Transfer to an electric spice mill or pestle and grind until a coarse powder forms; set aside. Heat the oil in a *kaдai* or wok. Add the onions and stir-fry until golden brown. Stir in the garlic paste and continue stir-frying until the aroma of cooked garlic is evident. Add the tomatoes, chillies and ginger and continue stir-frying until the fat separates. Add the ground masala, the tomato purée/paste and chicken pieces and continue stir-frying until the fat separates again and the chicken is cooked through and tender. Sprinkle with lemon juice, fenugreek leaves, garam masala and the salt. Serve hot garnished with coriander/ cilantro.

ANDHRA FRIED CHICKEN
Fried Chicken, Andhra Pradesh Style

SEE PHOTOGRAPH ON PAGE 137

THIS SUCCULENT, spicy fried chicken dish is a speciality of the Anarkali Restaurant, in Andhra Pradesh. I flew there once specifically to try this and some other dishes. From that tasting session, I created this dish for the restaurant. A couple of regular guests always ring ahead to request this when they are coming to dine.

SERVES 4

2 chickens, each about 1.1 kg/2½ lb, skinned and cut into 10 pieces

juice of 1 lemon

2 raw eggs

1½ tablespoons Kashmiri red chilli powder or cayenne pepper

1½ tablespoons Ginger and Garlic Paste (page 29)

2 teaspoons ground cumin

1 teaspoon turmeric

1 teaspoon dry fenugreek leaves

1 teaspoon Garam Masala (page 28)

salt, to taste

vegetable oil for frying

2 teaspoons shop-bought chaat masala

chopped fresh coriander/cilantro leaves, to garnish

MIX TOGETHER the chicken, lemon juice, eggs, chilli powder, ginger and garlic paste, ground cumin, turmeric, fenugreek leaves, garam masala and salt. Leave to marinate for at least 1 hour at room temperature or longer in the refrigerator.

Heat enough oil to fry the chicken in a *kaдai* or wok until it is about 180°C/350°F, or until a cube of bread will brown in about 45 seconds. Add the chicken pieces and fry for 12–15 minutes until cooked through and tender: test one piece by cutting through – it should be crisp on the outside and the juices should run clear. Serve the chicken straight from the *kaдai*, sprinkled with chaat masala and chopped coriander/cilantro leaves.

CHICKEN COONDAPURI
Chicken with a Special Regional Masala

I FOUND THIS RECIPE while I was working down South in Mangalore. A fellow chef took me to his village, and his mother cooked this for us. I begged her for the recipe, and as there was no name for it, I christened it after the village – Coondapur. The secret of this recipe is the ground spices you add to finish the cooking – they transform the whole dish. You can make up this masala in advance and store it in an airtight container. Two coconuts will make all the required coconut milk.

SERVES 4

1 chicken, about 1.5 kg/3½ lb, skinned, boned and cut into
4 cm/1½ inch cubes
450 ml/16 fl oz/2 cups thin coconut milk (page 32)
2 onions, chopped
juice of 1 lemon
salt, to taste
2 tablespoons vegetable oil
5 garlic cloves, chopped
3 tablespoons grated fresh coconut, about ¼ coconut, coarsely ground
225 ml/8 fl oz/1 cup thick coconut milk (page 32)
boiled rice, to serve

FOR THE COONDAPURI MASALA
12–15 dried red chillies
6 large garlic cloves, with the skins left on
1½ tablespoons coriander seeds
½ tablespoon black peppercorns
2 teaspoons turmeric
1 teaspoon fenugreek seeds

TO MAKE THE MASALA, dry-roast all the ingredients in a large frying pan/skillet until the spices are crisp. Transfer to an electric spice mill or pestle and blend until finely ground; set aside. Place the chicken in a glass bowl. Add the thin coconut milk, the dry masala mixture, half the chopped onions, lemon juice and salt and leave to marinate for 20 minutes.

Heat the oil in a large saucepan or flameproof casserole. Add the remaining onions and garlic and fry until brown. Add the ground coconut and continue frying for 1 minute until it turns light brown. Add the marinated chicken and all the juices from the bowl and bring to the boil. Lower the heat and simmer for about 15 minutes until the liquid evaporates and all the pieces are cooked through and tender. Stir in the thick coconut milk and simmer for a further few minutes until well blended. Serve, ideally with boiled rice.

MURGH PISTA KORMA
Chicken with Pistachios and Green Herbs

A SIGNATURE DISH of the Bombay Brasserie, and one of the most popular. It uses cashew nuts, almonds and, of course, pistachio nuts, which have to be individually peeled. In a domestic kitchen that's not too much of a chore – blanch then and rub them with kitchen paper/paper towels to remove the skins – but for the amount needed in the Brasserie, it's quite a job!

SERVES 4

75 g/3 oz/½ cup shelled pistachio nuts

75 g/3 oz/½ cup shelled cashew nuts

5 garlic cloves

1 onion, chopped

1 cm/½ inch piece of fresh root ginger, peeled and coarsely chopped

5 green chillies

4 sprigs fresh coriander/cilantro leaves

1 sprig fresh mint

1 large green pepper, cored, seeded and coarsely chopped

½ teaspoon cumin seeds

1 tablespoon vegetable oil

6 green cardamom pods

1 chicken, about 1.5 kg/3½ lb, skinned, boned and cut into 4 cm/1½ inch cubes

2 tablespoons single/light cream

1 teaspoon ground white pepper

1 teaspoon garam masala (page 28)

juice of ½ lemon

salt, to taste

chopped fresh coriander/cilantro and pistachio nuts, to garnish

SOAK THE PISTACHIO AND CASHEW NUTS in water to just cover for 30 minutes. Place the nuts and liquid in an electric blender and blend until a thick, smooth paste forms; set aside. Meanwhile, place the garlic, onion and ginger in a blender or food processor and process until a smooth paste forms, adding just enough water to help blend the ingredients, rather than thin them; set aside.

Clean out the blender. Add the chillies, coriander/cilantro, mint, pepper and cumin seeds and blend to a smooth paste, adding a little water if necessary; set aside. Heat the oil in a large saucepan. Add the cardamoms and fry until they are light brown. Stir in the onion paste and continue frying over a low heat until the aroma of fried onions and garlic is evident.

Stir in the green herb paste and fry for 2 minutes, then stir in the nut paste. Simmer for 5 minutes, then add the chicken pieces and 100 ml/4 fl oz/½ cup water. Stir together, then continue to simmer for 15–18 minutes until the chicken is cooked through and tender.

Add the cream, white pepper, garam masala, lemon juice and salt and simmer for a few more minutes. Serve garnished with chopped coriander/cilantro and pistachio nuts.

PREVIOUS SPREAD, clockwise from far left: Palak Pakodi Kadi (*page 146*); Rogini Murgh (*page 159*); Gosht Nu Pulao (*page 87*); Andhra Fried Chicken (*page 134*); Karwari Jhinga (*page 132*); Achar Gosht (*page 141*).

ROGINI MURGH
Fried Chicken Topped with a Moghlai Sauce

SEE PHOTOGRAPH ON PAGE 136

THIS IS MY VERSION of a classic recipe. Normally this would be a curry in a bowl, but I like to make it more interesting with extra eye appeal by topping the fried pieces with the sauce. It proved very popular at a prominent magazine's lunch party.

SERVES 4

15 cashew nuts
1 tablespoon poppy seeds
150 g/5 oz/1 cup Fried Brown Onions (page 32)
6–8 garlic cloves, peeled
1 cm/½ inch piece of fresh root ginger, peeled
1 tablespoon mild chilli powder or paprika
4 chicken breasts, skinned and boned, but with the wing bone left on
1 tablespoon lemon juice

1 teaspoon ground white pepper
½ teaspoon turmeric
salt, to taste   flour for dusting
3 tablespoons vegetable oil
200 ml/7 fl oz/scant 1 cup natural yogurt (page 33)
1 teaspoon garam masala (page 28)
salt, to taste
chopped fresh coriander/cilantro leaves, to garnish

SOAK THE CASHEWS and poppy seeds in 225 ml/8 fl oz/1 cup water for 30 minutes. Place the nuts, seeds and liquid in an electric blender and blend until a thick, smooth paste forms. Add the brown onions, garlic, ginger and chilli powder and blend until another paste forms; set aside.

Meanwhile, place the chicken breasts in a glass dish. Add the lemon juice, white pepper, turmeric and salt and leave to marinate for 15–20 minutes. Liberally dust the chicken breasts with flour. Heat the oil in a large frying pan/skillet over a low to medium heat. Add the chicken breasts and fry for 12–15 minutes until they are golden brown. Remove from the pan and set aside. Strain 1 tablespoon of the oil into a saucepan

and heat. Add the reserved paste mixture and fry for 1 minute, stirring. Stir in 450 ml/16 fl oz/2 cups water and simmer for 6–8 minutes, stirring frequently. Return the chicken to the pan and simmer for 8–10 minutes, sprinkling with water occasionally to prevent the masala from sticking to the bottom of the pan.

Transfer the chicken to a serving platter, but leave as much of the masala behind in the pan as possible. Stir in the yogurt, garam masala and salt and simmer for 3–4 minutes. The sauce should be coating consistency, so add a little water if necessary. Spoon over the chicken breasts and serve, garnished with coriander/cilantro.

CHICKEN KORMA NARANGI
Orange-Flavoured Chicken with Cashew Paste

THIS IS ESSENTIALLY a chicken *korma*. The idea for this recipe came about as I tried to find a dish for children not able to eat spicy food. I guess it worked because it is now one of the most popular dishes for kids – and grown-ups!

SERVES 4

30 cashew nuts

1 tablespoon vegetable oil

4 green cardamom pods

3 cloves

1 onion, chopped

1 cm/½ inch piece of cinnamon stick

4 green chillies, chopped

4 tablespoons Ginger and Garlic Paste (page 29)

450 ml/16 fl oz/2 cups natural yogurt (page 33)

1 tablespoon ground coriander

1 teaspoon ground cumin

1 teaspoon Kashmiri red chilli powder or cayenne pepper

1 chicken, about 1.5 kg/3½ lb, boned and cut into pieces

finely grated rind/peel and juice of 2 oranges

salt, to taste

finely shredded orange rind/peel

coriander/cilantro leaves, to garnish

SOAK THE CASHEW NUTS in water to just cover for 30 minutes. Place the nuts and liquid in an electric blender and blend until a thick, smooth paste forms; set aside. Heat the oil in a large *kadai* or wok. Add the cardamoms, cloves, onion and cinnamon and stir-fry until the onions are just light brown. Add the green chillies and the garlic and ginger paste and continue stir-frying until the aroma of cooked garlic is evident.

Gradually stir in the yogurt and continue cooking, stirring, until the fat separates. Add the cashew paste with the ground coriander and cumin and continue cooking until the fat separates again. Stir in 750 ml/1¼ pints/3 cups water.

Add the chicken and continue simmering for 35–40 minutes until all the pieces are cooked through and tender. Add extra water while the curry cooks if necessary. Stir in the orange rind and juice and salt. Serve hot, garnished with the orange shreds and coriander/cilantro.

KOSHA MANGSHO
Stir-Fried Marinated Lamb

THE TECHNIQUE FOR COOKING this is unique: you grind your masala, then put it in a covered pan with the potatoes, tomatoes and lamb and simultaneously everything cooks to perfection. This is a Bengali speciality of my mother, Uma Sarkhel.

SERVES 4

6 dried red chillies, or 1 tablespoon Kashmiri chilli powder or cayenne pepper

6 garlic cloves, peeled

4 green chillies

2 onions, quartered

2.5 cm/1 inch piece of fresh root ginger, peeled

1 tablespoons cumin seeds

900 g/2 lb leg or shoulder of lamb, or lamb chops

8 whole tomatoes

2 large potatoes, peeled and quartered

3 dried bay leaves

2 tablespoons mustard oil

salt, to taste

8 green cardamom pods, ground with the skins on

2.5 cm/1 inch piece of cinnamon stick, ground

1 tablespoon vinegar

1 teaspoon sugar

PLACE THE DRIED RED CHILLIES, garlic, green chillies, onions, ginger and cumin seeds in a pestle and grind until a smooth paste forms. Place the lamb in a large glass bowl. Stir in the masala paste, then add the tomatoes, potatoes, bay leaves, mustard oil and salt; set aside for 1 hour.

Transfer everything to a flameproof casserole with a tight-fitting lid. Cook over a medium heat, covered, for about 1 hour, stirring carefully occasionally so you don't break up the tomatoes; they should dissolve on their own. Add a little water if necessary. Stir in the crushed cardamom, cinnamon, vinegar and sugar. Serve hot.

ACHAR GOSHT
Lamb in Pickling Spices

SEE PHOTOGRAPH ON PAGE 136

THIS IS A COMBINATION of lamb, yogurt and spices that are similar to those used in northern Indian pickles. The idea is to stuff green chillies with the spices and then bake them with the other ingredients. It's a typical Hydrabadi dish, but I have adopted it to use the *panch phoran* mixture, instead of the cumin, fenugreek and mustard and onion seeds that are always included in authentic Hydrabadi recipes.

SERVES 4

2 tablespoons Panch Phoran (page 33)

8–10 green chillies, slit

900 g/2 lb leg of lamb, all fat removed, boned and cut into 2.5 cm/1 inch cubes

600 ml/1 pint/2½ cups natural yogurt (page 33)

3 onions, sliced

3 tablespoons mustard or vegetable oil

2 tablespoons ground coriander

1 tablespoon Ginger and Garlic Paste (page 29)

salt, to taste

Naans (page 69) or Laccha Paratha (page 72), to serve

PLACE THE *PANCH PHORAN* in a pestle and crush. Use half of this spice mixture to stuff the chillies. Place the remaining *panch phoran*, the lamb, yogurt, onions, oil, ground coriander, ginger and garlic paste and salt in a large flameproof casserole with a tight-fitting lid. Stir together and add the chillies.

Bring to the boil over a high heat, then lower the heat, cover and simmer for about 30 minutes. Sprinkle with a little water if necessary and transfer to an oven preheated to 220°C/425°F/Gas 7 and cook for 18–20 minutes until the lamb is tender and cooked through. Remove from the oven and serve hot with the bread.

ELAICHI GOSHT
Lamb Curry Flavoured with Black Cardamom

THIS IS ONE-SPICE COOKING – one clear flavour coming across, instead of a complex masala combination. I think black cardamom is the best spice to complement lamb, doing to lamb what dill does to fish. This is example of how a traditional dish can be varied a little – it is a lamb *korma* flavoured with cardamom.

SERVES 4

15 cashew nuts

1 tablespoon poppy seeds   2 tablespoons vegetable oil

3 dried bay leaves

seeds from 3 black cardamom pods

2 onions, sliced

2 tablespoons Ginger and Garlic Paste (page 29)

450 ml/16 fl oz/2 cups natural yogurt (page 33)

6 green chillies, chopped

1 tablespoon ground coriander   1 teaspoon ground cumin

1 kg/2¼ lb lamb, boned and cut into pieces

2 teaspoons ground green cardamom seeds

2 teaspoons ground black pepper

salt, to taste

2 tablespoons single/light cream

15 g/½ oz/1 tablespoon unsalted butter

chopped fresh coriander/cilantro, to garnish

SOAK THE CASHEWS and poppy seeds in water to just cover for 30 minutes. Place the nuts, poppy seeds and liquid in an electric blender and blend until a thick, smooth paste forms; set aside. Heat the oil in a large saucepan. Add the bay leaves and black cardamom seeds and fry for 30 seconds until they crackle. Add the onions and continue frying until they are light brown. Stir in the ginger and garlic paste and continue frying until the aroma of cooked garlic is evident.

Add the cashew and poppy seed paste, yogurt, chillies, ground coriander and ground cumin. Continue for 12–15 minutes until the mixture is reduced by half.

Stir in the lamb and cook for 5–6 minutes. Add enough water to just cover the lamb and continue simmering for 40–45 minutes until the lamb is cooked through and tender. Add extra water if necessary as the lamb cooks. Sprinkle with the ground cardamom, pepper and salt, then stir in the cream and butter. Stir for a minute, then serve garnished with coriander/cilantro.

GOSHT KANGARI
Mild Lamb Curry with Cheese

IN THE SOUTHERN HILL STATION of Ootacamund – known as Ooty during the British Raj – they made super cheese, very much like a mature English Cheddar. I developed this recipe to use Ooty cheese, and it is named after one of the small farms where the cheese was made. As Ooty isn't available in London, I use Cheddar and the result is just as successful.

SERVES 4

20 cashew nuts

4 green chillies

2 large onions, quartered   1 tablespoon poppy seeds

2 tablespoons vegetable oil

2 dried bay leaves

1 teaspoon green cardamom pods   1 small onion, finely chopped

1 tablespoon Ginger and Garlic Paste (page 29)

900 g/2 lb leg of lamb, trimmed of all fat, boned and cut into

2.5 cm/1 inch cubes

225 ml/8 fl oz/1 cup natural yogurt, whisked (page 33)

100 ml/4 fl oz/½ cup single/light cream

75 g/3 oz/¾ cup mild Cheddar cheese, grated

2 teaspoons ground white pepper

1 teaspoon Mace, Nutmeg and Green Cardamom Powder (page 29)

salt, to taste

chopped fresh coriander/cilantro leaves, to garnish

PLACE THE CASHEWS, chillies, onions, poppy seeds and 450 ml/ 16 fl oz/2 cups water in a saucepan and bring to the boil. Lower the heat and simmer, uncovered, for about 10 minutes until the onions are soft. Leave to cool, then transfer to an electric blender and blend until a fine paste forms; set aside. Heat the oil in a large flameproof casserole. Add the bay leaves and cardamoms and fry until the bay leaves just start to brown. Add the onion and fry until light brown. Stir in the ginger and garlic paste and fry until the aroma of cooked garlic is evident.

Add the lamb and stir-fry over a high heat for 4–5 minutes. When the liquid from the meat is oozing out, lower the heat and add the paste. Cover and simmer for 30–35 minutes, stirring occasionally and adding a little extra water if necessary.

Gradually stir in the yogurt and continue simmering for 15 minutes until the lamb is tender and cooked through. Stir in the cream, cheese, pepper, the mace, nutmeg and green cardamom powder and salt. Serve at once, garnished with coriander/cilantro.

NIZAM ROYAL BIRYANI
Lamb Chop Biryani

THIS IS A LAYERED BIRYANI, very popular with the Nizams of Hydrabad for holiday celebrations. I was fortunate to learn this speciality in Bombay at the President Hotel's Gulzar Restaurant. It is painstaking to prepare, but well worth the effort if your guests are food enthusiasts.

SERVES 4–6

750 g/1½ lb/3¾ cups basmati rice

25 g/1 oz/2 tablespoons butter   25 g/1 oz/2 tablespoons ghee

1½ tablespoons Ginger and Garlic Paste (page 29)

4 tablespoons natural yogurt (page 33), whisked

2 tablespoons ground coriander   1 tablespoon turmeric

12 pieces of 2-bone lamb chops, all fat trimmed

12 green chillies, sliced   3 large sprigs fresh mint, chopped

1½ tablespoons garam masala (page 28)

salt, to taste

450 g/1 lb/3 cups Fried Brown Onions (page 32)

2 tablespoons white distilled vinegar

1 tablespoon vegetable oil   2 teaspoons black cumin seeds

½ bunch fresh coriander/cilantro leaves, finely chopped

4 tomatoes, diced   pinch of saffron

2.5 cm/1 inch piece of fresh root ginger, peeled and cut into julienne sticks

450 ml/16 fl oz/2 cups milk, mixed with 1 tablespoon rice flour

WASH THE RICE by putting it in a large bowl and covering with water, then drain off the cloudy water. Repeat 3 or 4 times until the water remains clear. Cover with fresh water and leave to soak for 30 minutes. Melt the butter and ghee in a large saucepan. Add the ginger and garlic paste and fry, stirring constantly, for a few minutes until the aroma of fried garlic is evident. Gradually stir in the yogurt, then add the ground coriander and turmeric and simmer for 2–3 minutes. Add the lamb chops and stir-fry for 8–10 minutes until they are half cooked through. Stir in 100 ml/4 fl oz/½ cup water and continue simmering until the chops are cooked through and tender. Stir in the chillies, mint, ½ tablespoon of the garam masala and salt, then remove from the heat, cover and set aside.

Meanwhile, bring a large saucepan of water, about 3 times the volume of the rice, to the boil. Add 1 tablespoon of the browned onions, the vinegar, vegetable oil and black cumin. When the water is boiling, stir in the drained rice and return to the boil until the rice is half cooked. Test the rice by pressing a grain between your fingers: the centre should be white and powdery. Drain through a large sieve/strainer.

To assemble the biryani use a deep flameproof casserole with a tight-fitting lid; a small diameter is preferable. Arrange 4 chops and some of their gravy on the bottom. Sprinkle with a little of the remaining garam masala, one-third of the remaining brown onions, one-third of the coriander/cilantro, one-third of the tomatoes, a pinch of saffron, one-third of the ginger and a little of the milk. Top this with one-third of the rice. Make 2 more layers, using all the chops and rice. Add any remaining brown onions, milk and saffron to the top layer of rice. Cover with a wet piece of kitchen paper/paper towel; the water from the towel will help to create steam while the dish cooks. Cover and cook in an oven preheated to 220°C/425°F/Gas 7 for 20 minutes. Garnish with the coriander/cilantro and serve straight from the casserole.

144

SAI BHAJI Ⓥ
Greens, Vegetables and Lentils, Sindhi Style

SAI MEANS 'GREEN' IN SINDHI, and *bhaji* indicates a mix of vegetables. This dish comes from North-West India, and I first enjoyed it at the home of a Sindhi friend of my wife. I was taken up with its flavour and the balance of nutrients. This is a particularly good accompaniment to a vegetarian main course. I have prepared this for two Sindhi weddings in London using sorrel, instead of the more authentic, but difficult to get, sour spinach. The results are just as delicious.

SERVES 4

4 tablespoons yellow gram or channa dal
2 bunches spinach leaves, well rinsed, shaken dry and chopped
2 bunches sorrel leaves, rinsed and chopped
2 onions, finely chopped
1 large potato, peeled and finely chopped
1 large aubergine/eggplant, peeled and finely chopped
2 tablespoons vegetable oil   1 teaspoon cumin seeds
6 green chillies, chopped   3 tomatoes, chopped
1 cm/½ inch piece of fresh root ginger, peeled and chopped
1 teaspoon Kashmiri chilli powder or cayenne pepper
½ teaspoon turmeric   salt, to taste

PLACE THE YELLOW GRAM in a bowl with water to cover and set aside for 20 minutes. Place the yellow gram, spinach, sorrel, onions, potato and aubergine/eggplant in a saucepan with 450 ml/16 fl oz/2 cups water and bring to the boil. Lower the heat and simmer, uncovered, for about 25 minutes until the yellow gram is tender and most of the liquid evaporated.

Heat the oil in saucepan. Add the cumin seeds and fry until they crackle. Stir in the chillies, tomatoes, ginger, chilli powder and turmeric and stir-fry for 4–5 minutes. Add the spinach mixture and 225 ml/8 fl oz/1 cup water and continue simmering and stirring and mashing with a wooden spoon until all blended together. Adjust the seasoning and serve.

GOBI KA PATTICE Ⓥ
Cauliflower Cutlets

A BENGALI DISH from the repertoire of the highly respected Mog cooks of Assam, who were often chefs at the large tea plantations in North Bengal. Where I was born and grew up, in Jamshedpur, we had a Mog-run restaurant at the top of the hill, and this recipe was one of the specialities there.

MAKES 12

900 g/2 lb cauliflower, broken into florets
225 g/8 oz potato, peeled and quartered
100 g/4 oz/scant 1 cup plain/all-purpose flour
1 teaspoon crushed black peppercorns
salt, to taste
3 tablespoons vegetable oil
225 g/8 oz/1½ cups onions, chopped
1 quantity Chilli Chutney (page 44), to serve

BOIL THE CAULIFLOWER and potato in separate pans of boiling water until tender. Drain and finely chop the cauliflower, then leave to cool in the colander over the sink. Peel and mash the potato. Stir the flour into the mashed potato, then add the cauliflower, pepper and salt and stir together.

Heat 1 tablespoon of the oil in a large frying pan/skillet. Add the onions and fry until they are brown. Add the potato and cauliflower mixture into the pan and stir together, then remove from the pan. When cool enough to handle, form into 12 patties. Heat the remaining 2 tablespoons oil in the wiped-out frying pan/skillet. Shallow fry the patties, in batches, until golden brown on both sides. Drain well on crumpled kitchen paper/paper towels. Serve hot with chilli chutney.

PALAK PAKODI KADI Ⓥ
Spinach Fritters with Yogurt Sauce
SEE PHOTOGRAPH ON PAGE 136

THIS DISH WAS INSPIRED by a dinner I prepared for the Prince of Wales' Youth Trust at Warwick Castle, when spinach fritters were served as the first course. I added these fritters into a tempered yogurt sauce and the result was a wonderful combination of crisp fritters and a smooth, light sauce.

SERVES 4

1 bunch spinach, well rinsed, shaken dry and finely chopped
3 tablespoons gram flour
1 teaspoon of Kashmiri chilli powder or cayenne pepper
pinch of baking powder
salt, to taste
vegetable oil for deep-frying
750 ml/1¼ pints/3 cups natural yogurt (page 33)
1 teaspoon turmeric
½ teaspoon sugar
salt, to taste
1 tablespoon vegetable oil
½ teaspoon brown mustard seeds
2 green chillies, chopped
0.5 cm/¼ inch piece of fresh root ginger, peeled and finely chopped
chopped fresh coriander/cilantro, to garnish

PLACE THE SPINACH, 2 tablespoons of the gram flour, chilli powder, baking powder, salt and 2 tablespoons water in a bowl and mix together. Heat enough oil to deep-fry the fritters in a *kadai* or wok to 180°C/350°F, or until a cube of bread browns in about 45 seconds. Use a dessertspoon to scoop up and drop small balls of the spinach mixture into the fat, working in batches, and fry until crisp and golden brown.

Remove from the pan and drain well on crumpled kitchen paper/paper towels. You should get 15–18 fritters. Whisk together the yogurt, remaining gram flour, turmeric, sugar and salt; set aside.

Heat the oil in a saucepan. Add the mustard seeds and fry until they crackle. Add the chillies and ginger and fry for 1 minute, stirring occasionally. Stir in the yogurt mixture and continue simmering for 15 minutes over a low heat, stirring occasionally. Adjust the salt in the yogurt mixture if necessary. Stir in the fritters and serve at once, garnished with coriander/cilantro.

MASALA BHAAT Ⓥ
Spiced Vegetable Pulao

SEE PHOTOGRAPH ON PAGE 112

THIS STYLE OF COOKING RICE produces very aromatic dishes. It contains all the natural goodness of the grains and combines the carbohydrates in the rice with vegetables – a meal on its own. At the Brasserie, you will regularly find a range of these mixed vegetable pulaos on our buffet menu. For a simpler dish, make it with just aubergines, mushrooms or potatoes . . . the list can go on and on.

SERVES 4

450 g/1 lb/2¼ cups basmati rice

4 tablespoons vegetable oil

10 curry leaves, optional

5 green cardamom pods

3 dried bay leaves

2.5 cm/1 inch piece of cinnamon stick

1 teaspoon cumin seeds

1 teaspoon black peppercorns

2 green chillies, finely chopped

1 large onion, finely chopped

2.5 cm/1 inch piece of fresh root ginger, peeled and finely chopped

100 g/4 oz/⅔ cup cauliflower, cut into small florets

100 g/4 oz/scant 1 cup shelled green peas

100 g/4 oz/scant 1 cup carrots, peeled and diced

100 g/4 oz/scant 1 cup green beans, stringed and chopped

1 tablespoon ground coriander

2 teaspoons Kashmiri red chilli powder or cayenne pepper

2 teaspoons turmeric

15 g/½ oz/1 tablespoon butter

salt, to taste

½ coconut, grated, to garnish

chopped fresh coriander/cilantro leaves, to garnish

WASH THE RICE by putting it in a large bowl and covering with water, then stir and drain off the cloudy water. Repeat 3 or 4 times until the water remains clear. Cover with fresh water and leave to soak for 30 minutes. Heat the oil in a large flameproof casserole with a tight-fitting lid. Add the curry leaves, cardamoms, bay leaves, cinnamon, cumin seeds and peppercorns and fry for 2 minutes. Add the chillies, onion and ginger and continue frying until the onions turn brown. Add the cauliflower, peas, carrots and beans to the casserole and stir-fry for 2 minutes. Add the ground coriander, chilli powder and turmeric and continue stir-frying for a further 2 minutes.

Stir in the butter and drained rice and stir so all the ingredients are well blended. Add the salt and enough water to come 2.5 cm/1 inch above all the ingredients. Leave to simmer until most of the water is absorbed, stirring a couple of times. Cover the casserole and cook in an oven preheated to 220°C/425°F/Gas 7 for 15–16 minutes. Remove from the oven and sprinkle the coconut over the rice. Use a spatula to loosen the rice grains a bit, then sprinkle with coriander/cilantro and serve.

ALOO DUM KASHMIRI Ⓥ
Potatoes, Kashmiri Style

TYPICAL OF ANY RECIPE described as being prepared in the Kashmiri style, this includes yogurt, brown onions and ground ginger. *Dum* in a recipe title means the dish is covered while it slowly simmers.

SERVES 4

1 kg/2¼ lb new potatoes, peeled

vegetable oil for deep-frying

250 ml/9 fl oz/heaped 1 cup natural yogurt (page 33)

1 teaspoon ground green cardamom pods

1 teaspoon ground cinnamon

3 tablespoons ghee, melted

1 tablespoon Ginger and Garlic Paste (page 29)

1 teaspoon Kashmiri red chilli powder or cayenne pepper

1 teaspoon turmeric

50 g/2 oz/½ cup Fried Brown Onions (page 32), ground to a paste in an

electric spice mill

salt, to taste

1 teaspoon crushed cumin seeds

1 teaspoon crushed fennel seeds

2 teaspoons ground dried ginger

chopped fresh coriander/cilantro leaves, to garnish

USE THE TIP OF A KNIFE to make incisions all over the potatoes. Heat enough vegetable oil to fry the potatoes in a deep saucepan to 220°C/425°F, or until a cube of bread browns in about 30 seconds. Add the potatoes and deep-fry, in batches if necessary, until golden brown. Drain on crumpled kitchen paper/paper towels; set aside.

Combine the yogurt, cardamom and cinnamon in a saucepan and whisk together. Place over a low heat and stir until the mixture comes to the boil; it is important to stir constantly or the yogurt will curdle.

Melt the ghee in a saucepan. Add the ginger and garlic paste and fry until the aroma of garlic is evident. Lower the heat, stir in the yogurt and simmer for about 20 minutes, stirring frequently. Stir in the chilli powder and turmeric and continue simmering over a low heat for a further 10 minutes. Add the potatoes to the pan, then stir in the fried brown onions and salt. Continue simmering until the potatoes are heated through. If the gravy is too thick, add a little water. Rub the cumin seeds in your palms and sprinkle it with the fennel seeds and ground dried ginger over the potatoes and gravy. Serve garnished with the coriander/cilantro.

CHOLAR DAL Ⓥ
Yellow Split Gram with Coconut and Raisins

THIS IS A FAVOURITE at Bengali weddings and Sunday lunches. The tempering is quite sweet. It goes particularly well with Puris (page 155).

SERVES 4 AS AN ACCOMPANIMENT

400 g/14 oz/2 cups split yellow gram or channa dal, well rinsed and drained

1 teaspoon turmeric

salt, to taste

chopped fresh coriander/cilantro leaves, to garnish

FOR THE TEMPERING

1 tablespoon vegetable oil

1 teaspoon Panch Phoran spice mixture (page 33)

¼ fresh coconut, peeled and cut into 0.5 cm/¼ inch dice

1 dried red chilli

2 teaspoons raisins

½ teaspoon sugar

PUT 1.2 LITRES/2 PINTS/5 CUPS water in a large saucepan. Add the lentils, turmeric and salt and bring to the boil.

Lower the heat and simmer, skimming the surface as necessary, until the lentils are soft. This dish is intended to be quite thick, so remove from the heat when the lentils are soft, but not mushy; set aside while preparing the tempering.

For the tempering, heat the oil in a *kadai* or wok. Add the *panch phoran* and fry until the mustard seeds crackle. Add the coconut and continue frying until it is light brown, then add the chilli, raisins and sugar. (Break the chilli in half if you want some extra heat.) Fry, stirring, until the raisins bloat up. Pour the *dal* into the *kadai* and stir together. Serve garnished with coriander/cilantro.

SHIKAR DISHES – THE FOOD OF THE HUNT

THE *SHIKAR*, OR ROYAL SHOOT, was an Indian princely tradition, which the British took to as happily as ducks to water. An expert chef would accompany the *shikaris* (hunters) to prepare the game in the wild. Being able to cook game to perfection was considered a great skill and a chef's reputation depended on it. Game in India would generally be deer, rabbit, wild pigeon, quail and wild duck. I have eaten tortoise meat and eggs prepared by my paternal uncles – but the recipes and memories are very faint, as I was only about nine years old. Game hunting and cooking in India has dropped noticeably in the past several decades, since everyone is increasingly aware of wildlife conservation.

The Bombay Brasserie had a small selection of *shikar* dishes on a previous menu; now these are prepared on request.

BATER MASALA DHUNGAR
Quails with Spices Smoked with Ghee

THIS DISH IS PREPARED in the Dhungar style. Traditionally a chef will put an onion skin (or a leaf if he's out with a hunting party) over the food, place a hot charcoal on it and pour over a little ghee to create smoke. The dish is then covered, so the smoke permeates the food to create a wonderful flavour. To re-create this at home, the charcoal will reach the correct smouldering temperature if you heat it in a tray under a hot grill/broiler, or use a pair of tongs to hold it over a gas flame.

SERVES 4

8 quails, skinned, cleaned and well rinsed

juice of 1 lemon

salt, to taste

1 tablespoon vegetable oil

3 garlic cloves, chopped

1 large onion, chopped

1 tablespoon ground coriander

1 tablespoon gram flour

2 teaspoons Kashmiri red chilli powder or cayenne pepper

2 teaspoons turmeric

1 teaspoon ground cumin

6 tomatoes, chopped

1 tablespoon natural yogurt (page 33)

2 sprigs fresh mint, finely chopped

25 g/1 oz/2 tablespoons ghee

½ onion skin

2–3 cloves

chopped fresh coriander/cilantro leaves, to garnish

SPRINKLE THE QUAIL with half the lemon juice and salt; set aside. Heat the oil in a deep flameproof casserole with a tight-fitting lid. Add the garlic and onion and fry until they become light golden brown. Add the ground coriander, gram flour, chilli powder, turmeric and ground cumin and continue frying, stirring occasionally, for about 3 minutes until the gram flour starts to darken. Add the tomatoes and natural yogurt and simmer, stirring constantly, for 2 minutes until well blended.

Place the quail in the pan and bring the masala mixture to the boil, then stir in 450 ml/16 fl oz/2 cups water and return to the boil. Lower the heat, cover and simmer for 18–20 minutes, moving the quail around gently occasionally. Stir in the remaining lemon juice, the mint and salt. Remove from the heat.

Melt the ghee in a ladle. Place the onion skin, or a small metal container, on top of the quail and masala. Place the hot charcoal (see Introduction) in this, add the cloves and pour over the melted ghee. Immediately cover the casserole and set aside for 15 minutes; some smoke may escape from the side of the casserole. Remove the onion skin, charcoal and cloves. Stir the ghee into the masala. Serve garnished with coriander/cilantro. As you eat, you get a wonderful smoky aroma of cloves and ghee.

HIRAN KI NEHARI
Stewed Venison

AT THE BRASSERIE we use shank of venison for this dish, but in classical Indian cooking a dish prepared Nehari style uses every part of the animal – the tongue, the knuckles, the brain, the neck . . . Traditionally, all the parts are made into a stew and left overnight in a pot sealed with a flour paste and covered with hot charcoal. This then serves as an early-morning breakfast for hunters.

SERVES 4

1.1 kg/2½ lb boneless venison leg or shank meat, trimmed and cubed

900 g/2 lb venison leg bones, chopped into 5 cm/2 inch pieces

6 green cardamom pods

6 cloves

4 whole green chillies

4 black cardamom pods

4 pieces of mace

1 head of garlic, peeled

1 large onion, sliced

2.5 cm/1 inch piece of fresh root ginger, peeled

45 g/1½ oz/3 tablespoons, ghee

2 onions, finely sliced

2 tablespoons Ginger and Garlic Paste (page 29)

1 tablespoon Kashmiri red chilli powder or cayenne pepper

1 tablespoon ground coriander

2 teaspoons turmeric

6 green chillies, chopped

1 tablespoon gram flour and 1 tablespoon plain/all-purpose flour mixed to a paste with 225 ml/8fl oz/1 cup water

4 tomatoes, chopped

2 teaspoons Mace, Nutmeg and Green Cardamom powder (page 29)

salt, to taste

1 green chilli, sliced, to garnish

1 cm/½ inch piece of fresh root ginger, peeled and cut into julienne sticks, to garnish

chopped fresh coriander/cilantro leaves, to garnish

PLACE THE VENISON and bones in a large stockpot or saucepan. Add the green cardamom, cloves, green chillies, black cardamom, mace, garlic, onion and ginger and enough water to cover.

Bring to the boil, skimming the surface as necessary, then lower the heat and simmer for about 50 minutes until the venison is cooked through and almost tender. Remove the meat from the pan with a slotted spoon; set aside. Simmer the bones and the flavouring ingredients in the pan for about 1 hour longer. Strain and add water if necessary to make up to 1.3 litres/2¼ pints/6 cups; set aside.

Melt the ghee in a large flameproof casserole with a tight-fitting lid. Add the onions and fry until they are crisp and golden brown. Stir in the ginger and garlic paste, chilli powder, ground coriander and turmeric and continue frying until the aroma of cooked garlic is evident. Add the chopped chillies with the flour paste and fry for 2 minutes. Add the tomatoes and continue frying for 3 minutes. Stir in the stock and venison and bring to the boil. Sprinkle with the mace, nutmeg and green cardamom powder. Add salt. Cover and cook in a oven preheated to 200°C/400°F/Gas 6 for 15–18 minutes. Serve garnished with the sliced chillies, ginger juliennes and coriander/cilantro.

Fresh Coconut
on Almonds and Cashew Nuts

Desserts

IN EVERY CORNER OF INDIA people have a sweet tooth. The two main types of sweet are those made from condensed milk, and sweets that have been fried in pure *ghee* (clarified butter). Bengal has its milk sweets, while in South India you'll find all the rice-based puddings. In Maharashtra, the sweets are typically made of yogurt and stuffed flour dumplings. Sweetmeat shops abound in Bombay – there are Maharashtrian, South Indian, and Bengali, as well as North Indian shops doing their famous *halwas*.

You might even find sweetmeats topped with *warak*. In Hydrabad, there is a whole street with craftsmen painstakingly beating silver or gold with tiny mallets to get superfine leaves of precious metals, which are used to cover the *halwas* and are eaten along with them. I spent a very eventful afternoon with one craftsman and proudly returned to Bombay with a sheet of silver *warak*, which I still cherish.

The art of sweet making in India is very specialized. Certain dishes can be made at home, but other Indian sweetmeats take special skill. Even in a small restaurant in Bombay you'd have a *halwai*, a person trained to make sweets like *kulfi*, the Indian condensed-milk ice cream. If you are entertaining and you want to round off your Indian meal with a traditional Indian sweet like *gulab jamum*, you can always buy them from sweetmeat shops in Indian areas – it's something I do myself. The recipes that follow are for sweets that are easy to make at home. Why not try them?

153

PAYESH Ⓥ
Rice Pudding

RICE PUDDING IS ENJOYED all over India with slight variations. *Kheer* is well known in northern India, as is *payasam* in the South. This recipe, however, is the creamy version made the Bengali way. At the Brasserie we take it in turns to feature the regional variations. Broken rice is sold in Asian grocery shops, but if you can't find any, put some uncooked basmati rice in a food processor and use the pulse button several times until it is broken into smaller pieces. Do not substitute short-grained pudding rice.

SERVES 4

225 g/8 oz/heaped 1 cup broken rice, well rinsed
2 litres/3½ pints/8¾ cups whole milk
2 tablespoons sugar, or more as required
6 green cardamom pods, split and crushed
12–15 seedless raisins
1 tablespoon cashew nuts

PUT THE RICE in a bowl, cover with water and leave to soak for 20 minutes. Meanwhile, place the milk in a saucepan and bring to the boil. Lower the heat and simmer, stirring and skimming the surface frequently, for 40–45 minutes until reduced by about one-quarter. Stir in the drained rice and sugar and return to the boil. Lower the heat and simmer again. Add the cardamoms, raisins and cashew nuts and continue simmering until the rice is tender; the total cooking time will be about 90 minutes. Use a wooden spoon and break up the grains as you stir. Do not scrape the bottom of the pan. Transfer to a glass bowl and serve hot, or leave to cool and chill until required.

SOOJI HALWA Ⓥ
Semolina in Syrup with Saffron

SEE PHOTOGRAPH ON PAGE 156

SEMOLINA IS USED all over India to make sweetmeats, such as *halwa*, *sheera* or savoury *upma*, or for coating ingredients before they are fried, such as breadcrumbs are used in Western kitchens. This recipe is very popular as an offering to gods during religious ceremonies. Semolina will usually be found in one form or another in the lunch buffet at the Brasserie.

SERVES 4

1½–2 tablespoons sugar, to taste
¼ teaspoon saffron
25 g/1 oz/2 tablespoons ghee
7.5 g/¼ oz/½ tablespoon salted butter
225 g/8 oz/1½ cups semolina
8–10 cashew nuts
1 tablespoon seedless raisins
1 teaspoon ground cardamom

PLACE THE SUGAR and saffron in a pan with 350 ml/12 fl oz/1½ cups water and stir to dissolve. Bring to the boil, then lower the heat and simmer for 15 minutes until a thin syrup forms. The syrup should be pouring consistency.

At the same time, melt the ghee and butter in a *kadai* or wok. (The salted butter helps to bring out the flavours of fried semolina and saffron.) Add the semolina and cook over a low heat, stirring constantly, for 10–12 minutes until it is golden brown and the aroma of fried semolina is evident. Add the syrup, cashews, raisins and ground cardamom to the semolina. Increase the heat to medium and stir-fry for 4–5 minutes. Serve hot or chilled – both are equally delicious.

SHAHI PARCHE ⓥ
Bread Pudding, Indian Style

SEE PHOTOGRAPH ON PAGE 157

Shahi parche, double ka meetha and *shahi tukra* are all synonymous with bread puddings, and they come from the kitchens of Hydrabadi Nizams. In fact, I was taught this recipe in Hydrabad by Ammi, the mother of my then chef colleague, Latafat Ali. This recipe must be decades old, as she was quite elderly when she taught me in 1985.

SERVES 4

20 blanched almonds

2 tablespoons shelled pistachio nuts

25 g/1 oz/2 tablespoons ghee

6 medium slices white bread, crusts removed and cut into triangles

2 eggs

4 tablespoons double/heavy cream

1–1½ tablespoons sugar, to taste

1 teaspoon Mace, Nutmeg and Green Cardamom Powder (page 29)

½ teaspoon saffron

extra almonds and pistachio nuts, to decorate

PUT THE ALMONDS and pistachio nuts in a bowl with just enough water to cover and leave for 30 minutes. Transfer the nuts and liquid to an electric blender and blend until a smooth, thick paste forms. Melt the ghee in a *kadai* or wok. Add the bread triangles and fry until they are golden brown. Transfer to a colander and leave to drain; reserve the ghee that drips off.

Mix together the nut paste, eggs, cream and sugar and beat until light and frothy. Warm the reserved ghee, nutmeg, mace and green cardamom powder and saffron. Whisk in the cream mixture. Arrange the fried bread slices in a greased ovenproof dish. Pour over the egg mixture. Bake in an oven preheated to 190°–200°C/375°–400°F/Gas 5–6 for 18–20 minutes until a light brown crust forms on the top. Sprinkle with extra nuts and serve.

SRIKHAND PURI ⓥ
Thick Sweetened Yogurt with Fried Bread

SEE PHOTOGRAPH ON PAGE 156

SERVES 4

900 ml/1½ pints/3¾ cups natural yogurt (page 33)

10 green cardamom pods, shelled with seeds ground in a pestle

4–5 tablespoons sugar, to taste

½ teaspoon saffron dissolved in warm milk

1 tablespoon chopped pistachio nuts, to decorate

½ tablespoon sunflower seeds, to decorate

FOR THE PURIS

450 g/1 lb/3 cups plain/all-purpose flour

salt, to taste   2 teaspoons vegetable oil

extra vegetable oil for deep-frying

PLACE THE YOGURT in a double thickness of muslin/cheesecloth and suspend over your sink for at least 8 hours until all the whey drips away and the yogurt is very thick. Transfer the yogurt to a bowl and stir in the cardamom seeds, sugar and saffron. Whisk constantly with a wire whisk for 15–20 minutes. Cover and chill for at least 30 minutes before serving. Serve decorated with the pistachio nuts and sunflower seeds.

Meanwhile, to make the puris, sift the flour and salt into a bowl and make a well in the centre. Add about 225 ml/8 fl oz/ 1 cup water, little by little, kneading until a firm dough forms. Cover with a warm, wet towel and leave to rest for 5 minutes. Knead the oil into the dough. Cover again and leave to rest for 10 minutes. Divide the dough into 12 equal balls and roll out very thinly on a lightly floured surface. Heat the oil for deep-frying in a *kadai* or wok to 180°C/350°F, or until a cube of bread browns in about 45 seconds. Fry one puri at a time for 40–45 seconds; it should puff up at once. Transfer to a colander to drain, then place another puri in the *kadai*. Continue until all are cooked. Do not be tempted to cook more than one at a time because they can become too brown before you can remove them. Serve the puris hot with the sweetened yogurt.

PARSI MITHOO SEV ⓥ
Vermicelli with Nuts, Parsi Style
SEE PHOTOGRAPH ON PAGE 156

THESE TWO RECIPES use *semiyan* or vermicelli. In this recipe the thin noodles are fried, simmered and finally baked. Parsis would normally have this with set sweetened yogurt. This is one of the most requested desserts for Parsi gatherings and celebrations here at the Brasserie.

Charoli nuts are tiny, round and brown, and sold at Asian grocery stores.

SERVES 4

2 tablespoons ghee
450 g/1 lb vermicelli, broken up
2 teaspoons charoli nuts
2 tablespoons sugar
6 almonds, sliced
1 tablespoon pistachio nuts, sliced
1 tablespoon seedless raisins
3 drops vanilla essence/extract
pinch of freshly grated nutmeg
extra chopped pistachio nuts, to decorate

MELT THE GHEE in a flameproof casserole with a tight-fitting lid. Add the vermicelli and charoli nuts and stir-fry over a medium heat until golden brown. Stir in the sugar, almonds, pistachio nuts, raisins, vanilla and nutmeg. Add about 225 ml/8 fl oz/1 cup water, a little at a time, until all the liquid is absorbed, stirring constantly. Bake in an oven preheated to 190°C/375°F/Gas 5 for 15 minutes. Serve hot garnished with pistachio nuts.

PREVIOUS SPREAD, clockwise from top left: Puris (*page 155*); Shrikand (*page 155*); Shahi Parche (*page 155*); Parsi Mithoo Sev (*page 158*); Sooji Halwa (*page 154*).

SEMIYAN PAYASAM ⓥ
Vermicelli with Milk

VERMICELLI ARE MADE FROM wheat and usually roasted or sun-dried before they come to market. Vermicelli has many uses at the Bombay Brasserie. As well as featuring in this dessert and a dry, Parsi-style dessert, it is used to give extra body to lamb and chicken curries. It can also be broken into small pieces and used to coat *pattices* before frying.

This recipe is made in the South Indian style. After you fry the vermicelli, the ghee can be strained through a fine sieve/strainer and used again.

SERVES 4

30 g/1 oz/2 tablespoons ghee
225 g/8 oz vermicelli, broken up
1 litre/1¾ pints/4½ cups whole milk
2 tablespoons sugar
1 tablespoon seedless raisins
8–10 cashew nuts
100 ml/4 fl oz/½ cup thick and thin coconut milks mixed together (page 32)
½ teaspoon ground cardamom seeds from fresh pods
chopped pistachio nuts, to decorate

MELT THE GHEE in a *kadai* or wok. Add the vermicelli and stir-fry them over a medium heat until they turn golden brown. Pour into a colander and leave to drain.

Place the milk in a large saucepan or flameproof casserole and bring to the boil. Add the sugar, raisins and cashews, lower the heat and simmer for 30–40 minutes until the milk is greatly reduced. (An easy way to do this without the milk sticking to the pan bottom or boiling over is to drop a small metal bowl into the pan. As the milk simmers, the bowl dances around, stirring the milk constantly. The bowl must be open-side down.) Remove the 'trick' bowl. Add the vermicelli, coconut milk and cardamom seeds and continue simmering until the vermicelli is soft. Serve hot, garnished with pistachio nuts.

INDEX

Page numbers in *italic* refer to illustrations